Greg Byrd, Lynn Byrd and Chris Pearce

Cambridge Checkpoint
Mathematics

Challenge Workbook

9

CAMBRIDGE
UNIVERSITY PRESS

University Printing House, Cambridge CB2 8BS, United Kingdom

One Liberty Plaza, 20th Floor, New York, NY 10006, USA

477 Williamstown Road, Port Melbourne, VIC 3207, Australia

314–321, 3rd Floor, Plot 3, Splendor Forum, Jasola District Centre, New Delhi – 110025, India

103 Penang Road, #05-06/07, Visioncrest Commercial, Singapore 238467

Cambridge University Press is part of the University of Cambridge.

It furthers the University's mission by disseminating knowledge in the pursuit of education, learning and research at the highest international levels of excellence.

www.cambridge.org
Information on this title: www.cambridge.org / 9781316637432 (Paperback)

First published 2017

20 19 18 17 16 15 14 13 12 11 10 9 8

Produced for Cambridge University Press by
White-Thomson Publishing
www.wtpub.co.uk

Editor: Sonya Newland
Designer: Ann Dixon
Illustrator: Ron Dixon

Printed in Great Britain by CPI Group (UK) Ltd, Croydon CR0 4YY

A catalogue record for this publication is available from the British Library

ISBN 978-1-316-63743-2 Paperback

··

Contents

Introduction

Welcome to Cambridge Checkpoint Mathematics Challenge Workbook 9

The *Cambridge Checkpoint Mathematics* course covers the Cambridge Secondary 1 Mathematics curriculum framework. The course is divided into three stages: 7, 8 and 9.

You can use this Challenge Workbook with Coursebook 9 and Practice Book 9. It gives you increasingly more difficult tasks or presents you with alternative approaches or methods in order to build on your existing skills.

Like the Coursebook and the Practice Book, this Workbook is divided into 19 units. In each unit there are exercises on each topic that will develop and extend your skills and understanding in mathematics. This will improve and deepen your understanding of the units. At the end of each unit are 'Mixed questions' to help you check your knowledge and understanding.

If you get stuck with a task:

• Read the question again.

• Think carefully about what you already know and how you can use it in the answer.

• Read through the matching section in the Coursebook.

1 Integers, powers and roots

1.1 Square roots and cube roots

Here is a way of finding a square root without using the square root button on a calculator.

To find $\sqrt{5}$

$2^2 = 4$, so the first estimate is 2.

Use the rule: next estimate $= \left(\text{last estimate} + \dfrac{5}{\text{last estimate}}\right) \div 2$

The second estimate is $\left(2 + \dfrac{5}{2}\right) \div 2 = 2.25$.

1 **a** Use a calculator to show that the second estimate is 2.25.

   b Use the rule to find the third estimate. Write down all the digits on your calculator.

   Third estimate = ...

   c Find the fourth estimate. Write down all the digits on your calculator.

   Fourth estimate = ...

   d How close is the fourth estimate to the value of $\sqrt{5}$ on your calculator?

   ....

2 **a** Use this method to make estimates of $\sqrt{28}$.

   First estimate ....

   Second estimate ....

   Third estimate ....

   Fourth estimate ....

   b How close is your fourth estimate to the calculator value for $\sqrt{28}$?

   ....

   c Explain why the calculator value for $\sqrt{28}$ is not exactly correct.

   ....

   ....

Here is a way to estimate the square root of a large number.

You want to estimate $\sqrt{5273514}$

Divide the number into pairs of digits starting from the right.

$$5 \mid 27 \mid 35 \mid 14$$

Look at the number on the left. The square root of 5 is between 2 and 3 and closer to 2.
Put one 0 for each other pair of digits: $2 \mid 0 \mid 0 \mid 0$

The estimate is $\sqrt{5273514} \approx 2000$

           $\approx$ means 'is approximately equal to'.

A calculator gives 2296.41..., so this estimate is correct to 1 s.f.

It is useful to make a quick estimate like this to check a calculator answer is correct.

3   Estimate the following square roots in the same way.

a $\sqrt{6872} \approx$ ....

b $\sqrt{91110} \approx$ ....

c $\sqrt{791833} \approx$ ....

d $\sqrt{5310} \approx$ ....

e $\sqrt{48000} \approx$ ....

f $\sqrt{480000} \approx$ ....

4   There is a similar way to estimate the cube root of a number. Describe the method, using $\sqrt[3]{7654321}$ as an example.

....

....

....

....

1.2 Working with indices

Here is a number: 2389.

The column headings for the digits are thousands, hundreds, tens and units.

$2389 = 2 \times 1000 + 3 \times 100 + 8 \times 10 + 9 \times 1$

You can write that as $2 \times 10^3 + 3 \times 10^2 + 8 \times 10^1 + 9 \times 10^0$.

Decimal numbers use powers of 10. Numbers that use powers of 2 instead of 10 are very important in computing. They are called binary numbers.

> Binary numbers only use two digits: 0 and 1.

Here is a binary number: 1011001.

What number is this?

$$1011001 = 1 \times 2^6 + 0 \times 2^5 + 1 \times 2^4 + 1 \times 2^3 + 0 \times 2^2 + 0 \times 2^1 + 1 \times 2^0$$
$$= 1 \times 64 + \quad 0 \quad + 1 \times 16 + 1 \times 8 + \quad 0 \quad + \quad 0 \quad + 1 \times 1$$
$$= \quad 64 \qquad\qquad + \quad 16 \quad + \quad 8 \qquad\qquad\qquad\quad + \quad 1$$
$$= \quad 89$$

The column headings for decimal whole numbers are one, ten, hundred, thousand, …

For numbers written in binary they are one, two, four, eight, sixteen, …

---

1 Write these binary numbers in decimal form.

a 1001 = ...

b 111 = ...

c 10101 = ...

d 1111 = ...

e 100100 = ...

f 101010 = ...

g 111000 = ...

h 1100011 = ...

Suppose you want to write 43 in binary form. Keep dividing by 2, like this, writing a remainder of 1 or 0 each time.

```
2 | 43
2 | 21   r 1   ↑
2 | 10   r 1   |
2 |  5   r 0   |
2 |  2   r 1   |
2 |  1   r 0   |
  |  0   r 1   |
```

Stop when you have zero at the bottom. Then write down the remainders from the bottom up: 43 = 101011.

Check: $43 = 1 \times 32 + 1 \times 8 + 1 \times 2 + 1 \times 1$.

2 Write these decimal numbers in binary. Put your divisions underneath.

a 22   **b** 53   **c** 83   **d** 100

22 = ...   53 = ...   83 = ...   100 = ...

You can also write fractions in binary. For example, 0.1 is $\frac{1}{2}$ and 0.01 is $\frac{1}{4}$.

3 Write these binary numbers as fractions.

a 0.11 = ...   **b** 0.101 = ...   **c** 0.0001 = ...   **d** 0.1111 = ...

Mixed questions

1 Without a calculator, work out estimates of these square roots.

a $\sqrt{53} \approx$ ....

b $\sqrt{530} \approx$ ....

c $\sqrt{5300} \approx$ ....

d $\sqrt{53000} \approx$ ....

2 **a** Show that 4^{-2} is the same as 2^{-4}.

....

b Show that 5^{-3} is NOT the same as 3^{-5}.

....

3 Write each of the following as a decimal.

a $8^{-1} =$ ......

b $5^{-2} =$ ......

c $20^{-1} =$ ......

4 **a** Write 4^3 as a power of 2. ....

b Write 8^3 as a power of 2. ....

c Write 4^{-3} as a power of 2. ....

5 The sum of two temperatures is 1 °C.

The difference between the temperatures is 20 °C.

Find the two temperatures.

....

...... and ......

6 Work out these roots. Write 'impossible' if they cannot be done.

a $\sqrt{-49}$ ....

b $\sqrt[3]{-27}$ ....

7 Work out these calculations.

a $3^2 + 3^{-2} =$ ....

b $3^2 \times 3^{-2} =$ ....

8 $2^{10} \approx 1000$

Use this fact to find the approximate value of each of these.

a $2^{-10} \approx$ ....

b $2^{20} \approx$ ....

2 Sequences and functions

2.1 Generating sequences

1 Here is a position-to-term rule:

term = (position number)^2 + 2 × position number – 1

You work out the fifth term in the sequence like this:

fifth term $= 5^2 + 2 \times 5 - 1$

$\qquad = 25 + 10 - 1$

$\qquad = 34$

Work out these terms in the sequence.

a First term

....

....

....

b Tenth term

....

....

....

2 Use the position-to-term rules to work out the first three terms and the tenth term of these sequences.

a term = (position number)^2 + 5 × position number + 3

....

....

....

....

....

....

b term = 3 × (position number)^2 – 2 × position number – 10

....

....

....

....

....

....

2.2 Finding the nth term

Look at this example of how to find the nth term of the sequence 3, 6, 11, 18, . . .

Term number (n)   1   2   3   4

Term   3   6   11   18

Difference   3   5   7

2nd difference   2   2

> Work out the difference between the terms, then work out the second difference. If the second difference is 2, then the formula for the nth term has n^2 in it.

n	1	2	3	4
n^2	1	4	9	16
	+2	+2	+2	+2
Term	3	6	11	18

So, the nth term is $n^2 + 2$.

> Make another table and start by working out the values of n^2, then compare the terms with the n^2 values. Decide what you need to add to the n^2 values to give you the terms.

1 Use the same method to work out the nth terms for each of these sequences.

a 5, 8, 13, 20, …

....

....

....

....

....

....

....

....

....

....

b 11, 14, 19, 26, …

....

....

....

....

....

....

....

....

....

....

c 2, 5, 10, 17, …

....

....

....

....

....

....

....

....

....

....

d 0, 3, 8, 15, …

....

....

....

....

....

....

....

....

....

....

2.3 Finding the inverse of a function

The equation for this function machine is $y = x^2 + 5$.

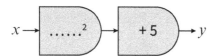

The inverse for this function is $x = \sqrt{y - 5}$.

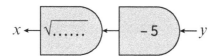

The inverse of squaring a number is to square root.

---

1 Work out the inverse function for each equation. Use the function machines to help.

a $y = x^2 + 4$

....

....

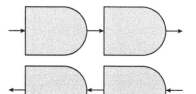

b $y = x^2 - 1$

....

....

c $y = 4x^2$

$4x^2$ is the same as $x^2 \times 4$.

....

....

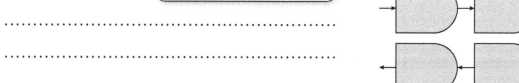

2 These cards show different mappings and their inverse functions.

$x \rightarrow 3x + 2$

$x \rightarrow \dfrac{x + 3}{2}$

$x \rightarrow \sqrt{\dfrac{x}{3}}$

$x \rightarrow x^2 + 3$

$x \rightarrow 3x^2$

$x \rightarrow \dfrac{x^2}{3}$

$x \rightarrow 2x + 3$

$x \rightarrow \sqrt{x - 3}$

$x \rightarrow 2x - 3$

$x \rightarrow \dfrac{x - 2}{3}$

$x \rightarrow \sqrt{3x}$

a Match each function to its inverse function.

....

....

....

....

....

....

....

....

....

....

....

....

Function	Inverse function

b There is one card left over. Write the inverse function for this mapping.

....

....

Mixed questions

In an **arithmetic sequence**, the term-to-term rule is either 'Add a number' or 'Subtract a number'. For example:

The term-to-term rule for the sequence 5, 7, 9, 11, ... is 'Add 2'.

The term-to-term rule for the sequence 10, 9, 8, 7, ... is 'Subtract 1'.

In a **geometric sequence**, the term-to-term rule is either 'Multiply by a number' or 'Divide by a number'. For example:

The term-to-term rule for the sequence 1, 2, 4, 8, ... is 'Multiply by 2'.

The term-to-term rule for the sequence 81, 27, 9, 3, ... is 'Divide by 3'.

1 Write down whether each of the sequences is an arithmetic sequence (AS) or a geometric sequence (GS). Write down the term-to-term rule and find the next term in each sequence.

a 4, 6, 8, 10, ...   AS or GS? ......

term-to-term rule: ......   next term: ......

b 2, 6, 18, 54, ...   AS or GS? ......

term-to-term rule: ......   next term: ......

c 40, 20, 10, 5, ...   AS or GS? ......

term-to-term rule: ......   next term: ......

d 65, 61, 57, 53, ...   AS or GS? ......

term-to-term rule: ......   next term: ......

2 Write down the first four terms of each of these geometric sequences.

a The first term is 2 and the term-to-term rule is multiply by 5.

....

b The first term is 800 and the term-to-term rule is divide by 4.

....

3 A ball is dropped from a height of 2 m. Each time it hits the ground, it bounces back up to half its previous height.

a Complete the table, showing the height after each bounce.

Bounce number	1	2	3	4
Height after bounce (cm)	100			

> The ball is dropped from a height of 200 cm, then bounces back to a height of 200 ÷ 2 = 100 cm.

b After which bounce will the height of the ball first be less than 4 cm?

....

....

3 Place value, ordering and rounding

3.1 Multiplying and dividing decimals mentally

1 Work out the areas of these shapes.

a

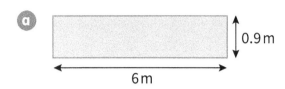

0.9 m

6 m

....

....

b

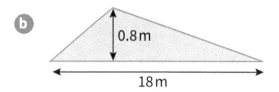

0.8 m

18 m

....

....

c

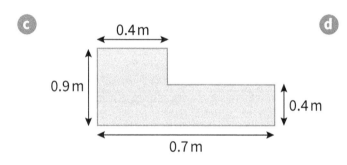

0.4 m

0.9 m

0.4 m

0.7 m

....

....

d

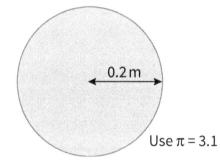

0.2 m

Use π = 3.1

....

....

2 A rectangle has an area of 0.32 m². The height of the rectangle is 0.08 m.
What is the length of the rectangle?

....

....

3 A circle has a perimeter of 2.17 m. What is the radius of the circle? Use π = 3.1.

....

....

4 Write 'True' or 'False' for each of these. If the answer is false, work out the correct answer.

a $0.4^2 = 0.16$ ....

b $1.2^2 = 1.44$ ....

c $0.05^2 = 0.025$ ....

d $\sqrt{0.09} = 0.03$ ....

e $\sqrt{1.69} = 1.3$ ....

f $(\sqrt{0.4})^2 = 0.4$ ....

3.2 Multiplying and dividing by powers of 10

1 **a** Put these cards into groups that give the same value.

A 450×10^{-1}

B 0.00045×10^4

C 0.45×10^0

D 0.45×10^2

E 4500×10^{-3}

F 4.5×10^{-2}

G 0.0000045×10^5

H 45×10^0

I 45×10^{-2}

J 0.45×10^1

....

....

....

....

....

b There is one card spare. Write two other cards that give the same value as this card.

> K

> L

3.3 Rounding

1 Use a calculator to work out these values. Round each answer to the given number of significant figures (s.f.) or decimal places (d.p.).

a 1.25^3

   i 2 d.p.   ....   **ii** 3 s.f.   ....

b π^2

   i 1 d.p.   ....   **ii** 1 s.f.   ....

c $\sqrt{2}$

   i 1 d.p.   ....   **ii** 5 s.f.   ....

2 A formula used in science is: $PE = mgh$

Work out PE when $m = 42$, $g = 9.8$ and $h = 125$. Give your answer to 2 s.f.

....

....

3 Another formula used in science is: $KE = \frac{1}{2}mv^2$

Work out KE when $m = 5.4$ and $v = 0.943$. Give your answer to 3 s.f.

....

....

4 Work out the area of this shape. Use $\pi = 3.142$.

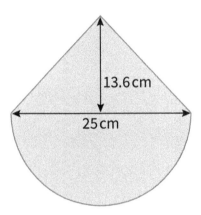

13.6 cm

25 cm

....

....

....

Give your answer to:

a 2 s.f ....

b 2 d.p. ....

3.4 Order of operations

1 Solve the clues to complete this puzzle. The first one has been done for you.

Clues:

Work out the value of the expressions when $a = 5$, $b = 9$, $c = 20$ and $d = 6$.

Down		Across	
1. $b^2 - 2d$	8. $(c - d)^2 + b$	1. $100d + \dfrac{ab}{3}$	11. $100(c - d - b) + a^2$
2. $(c + b - a)^2$	10. $10(b^2 - 2a)^2$	5. $(abc - d)^2$	14. $\left(\dfrac{cd}{2a}\right)^2$
3. $(2b - b^2)^2$	12. $b(a - c)^2$	6. $d(a + d)$	15. $9c - 9d$
4. $10(bc - 3d)$	13. $\dfrac{c^2 + d^2}{b - a}$	7. $\left(b + \dfrac{a}{c}\right) \times 10^3$	16. $(c(b + d))^2$
6. $2(b + d)^3$		9. $a(c^2 - b^2)$	

1. Down: $b^2 - 2d = 9^2 - 2 \times 6 = 81 \quad 12 = 69$

....

....

....

....

....

....

....

....

....

....

....

Mixed questions

1 Fill in the missing powers.

a 150,000 = 150 × 10 ......   **b** 82,000 = 820 × 10 ......

     = 15 × 10 ......   = 82 × 10 ......

     = 1.5 × 10 ......   = 8.2 × 10 ......

A number written in **standard form** is a number between 1 and 10 multiplied by 10 to a power. For example:

1.5×10^5 is written in standard form because 1.5 lies between 1 and 10.

15×10^4 is NOT written in standard form because 15 does not lie between 1 and 10.

2 Look at the numbers below. Put a tick (✓) next to the numbers that are written in standard form.

Put a cross (✗) next to the numbers that are not written in standard form.

a 4.5×10^3 ......

b 1.7×10^9 ......

c 32×10^5 ......

d 125×10^2 ......

e 2.99×10^8 ......

f 0.3×10^7 ......

3 Each of these numbers is written in standard form. Follow the example to write each of them as a normal number.

Example: $3.5 \times 10^3 = 3.5 \times 1{,}000 = 3{,}500$

Remember, $10^3 = 10 \times 10 \times 10 = 1000$.

a $2.7 \times 10^2 = $ ....

b $4.8 \times 10^4 = $ ....

c $1.25 \times 10^5 = $ ....

4 Circle the correct standard form number for each of these measurements.

a The mass of the Hubble Space Telescope is approximately 11 000 kg. This is the same as:

A 1.1×10^3 kg   **B** 1.1×10^4 kg   **C** 1.1×10^5 kg

....

b The distance from the Moon to Earth is approximately 384 000 km.
This is the same as:

A 3.84×10^5 km   **B** 3.84×10^4 km   **C** 3.84×10^3 km

....

c The distance from the Earth to the Sun is approximately 150 000 000 km.
This is the same as:

A 1.5×10^7 km   **B** 1.5×10^9 km   **C** 1.5×10^8 km

....

4.1 Solving problems involving measurements

In the UK, the height of a horse is measured in hands and inches.

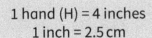
1 hand (H) = 4 inches
1 inch = 2.5 cm

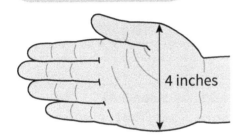

4 inches

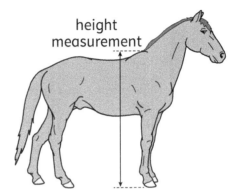

height measurement

A height measurement written as 15.2 H, means 15 hands and 2 inches.

A height measurement written as 11 H, means 11 hands and 0 inches.

1 Work out the height, in centimetres, of these horses. Complete the table.

> Convert the height in hands into inches first, then into centimetres.

Horse	Height in hands	Height in cm		Horse	Height in hands	Height in cm
Eagle	15.2 H			Jake	14.3 H	
Summer	16 H			Amazon	17.1 H	

....

....

....

....

....

2 A horse is fed a mixture of hay and hard feed, such as oats.

The amount of hay and hard feed a horse is fed depends on the type of work it does.

The table shows the ratio of hay : hard feed a horse should be fed when it does light, moderate or intense work.

Type of work	Hay : hard feed
light	3 : 1
moderate	3 : 2
intense	2 : 3

The total amount of food a horse should have each day is about 2% of its bodyweight.

Work out the amount of hay and hard feed each of these horses should be fed.

Complete the table.

Horse	Weight of horse (kg)	Type of work	Total amount of food (kg)	Amount of hay (kg)	Amount of hard feed (kg)
Eagle	500	moderate			
Summer	600	light			
Jake	450	moderate			
Amazon	720	intense			

....

....

....

....

....

....

....

....

....

4.2 Solving problems involving average speed

1 Hank is a delivery driver. He lives in Flagstaff, USA. On one day he delivers parcels to Sedona, Camp Verde and Winslow, then returns to Flagstaff.

The sketch map shows the positions of the towns and the distances between them in centimetres on the map.

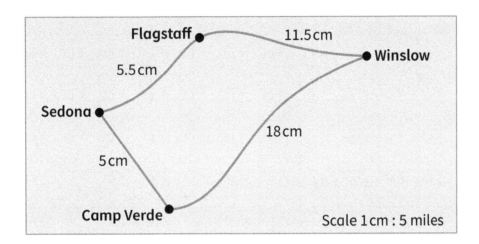

Hank leaves Flagstaff at 10 a.m. He spends 20 minutes in Sedona, 20 minutes in Camp Verde and 45 minutes in Winslow. He arrives back in Flagstaff at 3.25 p.m.

Work out his average speed for the time he is travelling. Give your answer in:

a miles per hour   **b** kilometres per hour   (Remember that 1 mile ≈ 1.6 km.)

....

....

....

....

....

....

....

....

....

4.3 Using compound measures

Density is a compound measure. It is the mass of a substance in a certain volume.

It is usually measured in grams per cubic centimetre (g/cm^3).

For example, rubber has a density of $1.5 \, g/cm^3$. This means that 1 cubic centimetre of rubber has a mass of 1.5 grams.

1 Rubber has a density of $1.5 \, g/cm^3$. Work out the mass of:

a $2 \, cm^3$ of rubber . . . .

b $5 \, cm^3$ of rubber . . . .

2 The table shows the density of different materials.

Material	Density (g/cm^3)		Material	Density (g/cm^3)		Material	Density (g/cm^3)
brass	8.6		ice	0.9		silver	10.5
copper	8.7		lead	11.4		wood (cedar)	0.4
gold	19.3		marble	2.6		wood (oak)	0.7

a Which material is the heaviest?   (The heaviest is the one with the greatest density.)

. . . .

b Which material is the lightest?

. . . .

c Work out the mass of $200 \, cm^3$ of marble.

. . . .

d Aaron puts four $1\,cm^3$ ice cubes in his drink. What is the mass of the ice?

....

e How much heavier is a necklace made from $2\,cm^3$ of gold than a necklace made from $2\,cm^3$ of silver?

....

....

f The diagram shows a wooden oak beam.

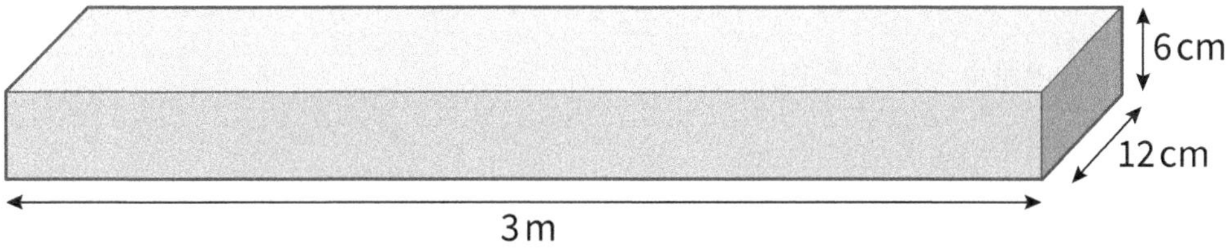

i Work out the volume of the beam in cm^3.

....

....

....

ii Work out the mass of the beam. Give your answer in kilograms.

....

....

....

....

Mixed questions

1 Here is a secret code box.

60	50	160	50	192	54		42	48	215	215	48	54	96	60

Work out the missing numbers from each of the statements below. Find the answer in the secret code box and write the letter that goes with the statement above the answer.

There are ...... minutes in $2\frac{2}{3}$ hours. (R)

There are ...... minutes in 3.2 hours. (N)

60 miles is the same as ...... km. (M)

15 m/s is the same as ...... km/h. (A)

A car travels 175 km in $3\frac{1}{2}$ hours. Its average speed is ...... km/h. (E)

Brass has a density of 8.6 g/cm^3. The mass of a 25 cm^3 piece of brass is ...... g. (L)

A cup holds 150 ml when full. ...... cups can be filled from a container holding 7.2 litres. (I)

12 g of gold costs $504. This is the same as $...... per gram. (W)

A car travels 18 km in 18 minutes. This is an average speed of ...... km/h. (S)

The answer is a famous sportsperson.

5 Shapes

5.1 Regular polygons

Here is a tessellation made from regular polygons.

At every vertex there are three triangles and two squares.

A symbol for the tessellation is 3.3.3.4.4

This means that as you go round any vertex, this is the order of the polygons.

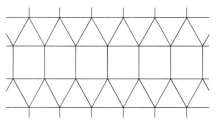

1. Draw the tessellation with the symbol 3.6.3.6

2. Draw the tessellation with the symbol 4.8.8

3 Draw the tessellation with the symbol 3.3.3.3.6

4 Find a tessellation that includes a 12-sided shape. Write down the symbol for it.

The symbol is ......

5.2 Symmetry of three-dimensional shapes

1 This is a square-based pyramid.

Show that it has four planes of symmetry. Your answer should include one or more diagrams.

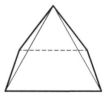

2 This is a cuboid.

How many planes of symmetry does it have? ......

Draw one or more diagrams to show them.

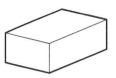

3 This is a prism. The cross-section is a regular hexagon.

How many planes of symmetry does it have? ......

Use diagrams to show them.

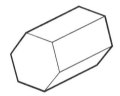

4 Every face of a cube is a square.

How many planes of symmetry does it have? ......

Use diagrams to show them.

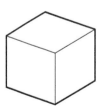

Mixed questions

1 **a** Five angles of a hexagon are 140°. What is the sixth angle? . . . .

b Explain why five angles of a hexagon cannot all be 145°.

....

c Explain why five angles of a hexagon cannot all be 108°.

....

d Sketch a hexagon where five of the angles are 90°.

2 Four identical cubes are joined together.

The plan, front elevation and side elevation are all the same shape.

Make an isometric drawing of the four cubes.

3 A square, an equilateral triangle and a regular pentagon meet at point P.

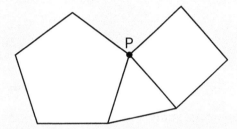

What regular polygons will fit in the gap remaining? Give a reason for your answer.

....

....

4 This shape is a regular pentagon.

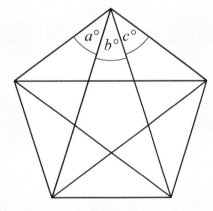

Show that angles a, b and c are all the same size.

....

....

....

....

6 Planning and collecting data

6.1 Identifying data

Investigation 1

Throughout this chapter, you are going to carry out an investigation.

Choose a topic that you are interested in – for example, music, sport, an activity or a hobby.

In this section (6.1) you are going to decide on a hypothesis, plan how to test it and write down any problems you may encounter. Complete the eight steps below.

1 Your hypothesis:

....

2 Questions you need to consider, or questions you will ask:

....

....

....

....

3 What data will you collect?

....

....

....

4 How will you collect the data?

....

....

....

5 What sample size will you use?

....

....

6 If your data involves a measurement, how accurate does your data need to be?

....

7 What other factors do you need to consider for your hypothesis?

....

....

....

8 What problems might you encounter?

....

....

6.2 Types of data

Investigation 2

1 Describe how you could collect primary data for your investigation (if possible).

....

....

....

....

2 Describe how you could collect secondary data for your investigation (if possible).

....

....

....

3 Which would be the best type of data for your hypothesis – primary or secondary? Explain your answer.

....

....

....

6.3 Designing data collection sheets

Investigation 3

1 Design a data collection sheet for your investigation.

....

....

....

....

....

....

....

....

....

....

....

6.4 Collecting data

Investigation 4

1 Carry out your survey and complete your data collection sheet from Section 6.3.

2 Write down at least one conclusion that you can make from the results of your survey.

....

....

....

....

....

....

3 Is the hypothesis you made at the start true or false? Explain your answer.

....

....

....

....

....

....

....

Mixed questions

Investigation 5

 1. Draw at least two charts or graphs to represent your data. You could choose to draw a bar chart, line graph, pictogram, pie chart, frequency diagram or another type of chart.

Remember to give your graphs or charts titles, to label the axes if appropriate and/or give them a key. You can use more paper if you need to.

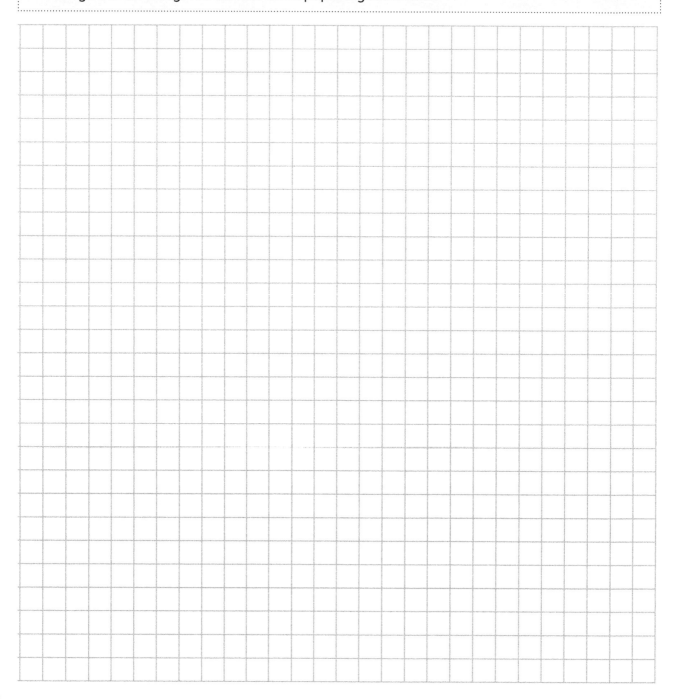

7 Fractions

7.1 Writing a fraction in its simplest form

1 The pie chart shows the composition of green gold. What fraction of green gold, in its simplest form, is:

a gold? . . . . . .

b silver? . . . . . .

c copper? . . . . . .

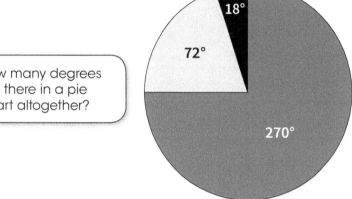

How many degrees are there in a pie chart altogether?

Composition of green gold

18°

72°

270°

◼ gold   ☐ silver   ◼ copper

2 The bar chart shows the composition of a piece of cheese. The total mass of the piece of cheese is 150 g.

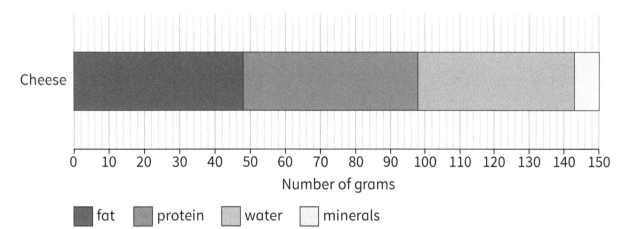

Composition of a 150g piece of cheese

Cheese

0 10 20 30 40 50 60 70 80 90 100 110 120 130 140 150
Number of grams

◼ fat   ◼ protein   ◻ water   ☐ minerals

What fraction of the cheese, in its simplest form, is:

a fat? . . . . . .

b protein? . . . . . .

c water? . . . . . .

d minerals? . . . . . .

3 The table shows the number of games won by each player in a tennis match.

	Set 1	Set 2	Set 3
Player A	6	3	7
Player B	3	6	5

What fraction of all the games in the match did Player A win? Write your answer in its simplest form.

....

....

7.2 Adding and subtracting fractions

1 The pie chart shows the proportion of workers of different ages at a factory.

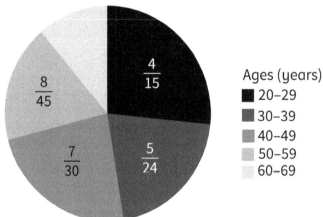

Ages of workers in a factory

Ages (years)
- ■ 20–29
- ■ 30–39
- ■ 40–49
- ■ 50–59
- ■ 60–69

a What fraction of the workforce are less than 40 years old?

....

....

b What fraction of the workforce are aged between 40 and 59?

....

....

c What fraction of the workforce are over 59 years old?

....

....

2 The diagram shows four fractions linked by lines.

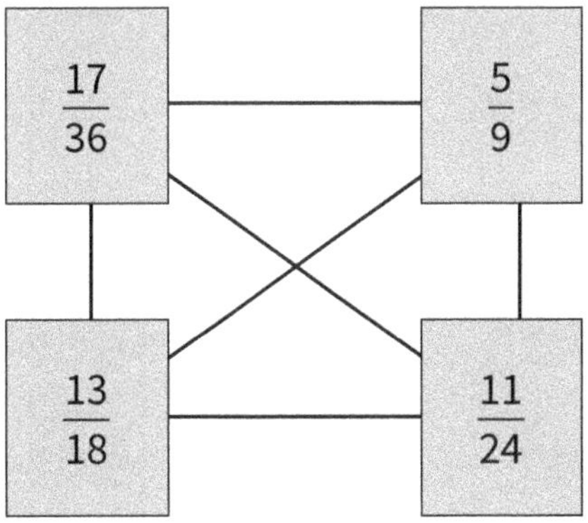

$$\frac{17}{36} \qquad \frac{5}{9}$$

$$\frac{13}{18} \qquad \frac{11}{24}$$

a Work out the total of any two of the linked fractions.

....

b Which two fractions give the greatest total? What is this total? Write your answer as a mixed number in its simplest form.

....

....

....

c Work out the difference between any two of the linked fractions.

....

d Which two fractions give the smallest difference? What is this difference? Write your answer in its simplest form.

....

....

7.3 Multiplying fractions

1 Work out the areas of these shapes. Give each answer as a mixed number in its simplest form.

a

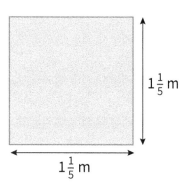

$1\frac{1}{5}$ m

$1\frac{1}{5}$ m

....

....

....

b

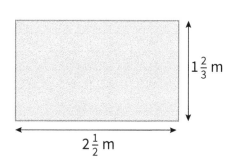

$1\frac{2}{3}$ m

$2\frac{1}{2}$ m

....

....

....

c

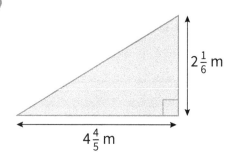

$2\frac{1}{6}$ m

$4\frac{4}{5}$ m

....

....

....

d

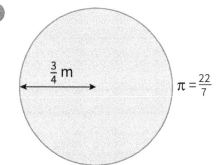

$\frac{3}{4}$ m

$\pi = \frac{22}{7}$

....

....

....

2 Work out the volume of this cuboid.

....

....

....

....

....

$1\frac{3}{4}$ m

$2\frac{4}{7}$ m

$5\frac{1}{3}$ m

7.4 Dividing fractions

1 The length of a rectangle is $3\frac{1}{3}$ m. The area is $9\frac{1}{6}$ m².

What is the width of the rectangle? Give your answer as a mixed number in its simplest form.

....

....

....

2 **a** Write the ratio $6\frac{1}{2} : 4\frac{1}{3}$ in the form $1 : n$, where n is a fraction in its simplest form.

> Remember that to write a ratio $A : B$ in the form $1 : n$, you need to divide both numbers by A. So $A : B = \frac{A}{A} : \frac{B}{A} = 1 : \frac{B}{A}$

....

....

....

b Write the ratio $5\frac{4}{5} : 4\frac{1}{7}$ in the form $n : 1$, where n is a mixed number in its simplest form.

....

....

3 It takes a chef $\frac{1}{4}$ of an hour to prepare 5 kg of vegetables.

How many vegetables can the chef prepare in $2\frac{1}{2}$ hours?

....

....

7.5 Working with fractions mentally

1. Look at the fraction snake. Using the numbers and symbols from the cloud, complete the workings in the snake. You can only use each number or symbol once.

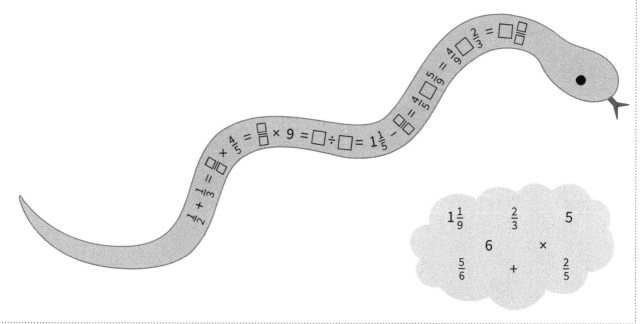

Snake workings:

$$\frac{1}{2} + \frac{1}{3} = \square\square \times \frac{4}{5} = \frac{\square}{\square} \times 9 = \square \div \square = 1\frac{1}{5} - \frac{\square}{\square} = \frac{4}{5} \frac{5}{9} = \frac{4}{9} \frac{2}{3} = \square \frac{\square}{\square}$$

Cloud:

$1\frac{1}{9}$ $\frac{2}{3}$ 5 6 $\times$ $\frac{5}{6}$ $+$ $\frac{2}{5}$

Mixed questions

1. Sort these cards into four sets of correct calculations. There must be one oval, one rectangular and one star-shaped card in each set.

Ovals: $\frac{4}{7}$ $2\frac{2}{5}$ $8\frac{3}{4}$ $1\frac{1}{2}$

Rectangles: $+3\frac{2}{3}$ $-2\frac{5}{6}$ $\times 1\frac{1}{2}$ $\div \frac{3}{14}$

Stars: $=3\frac{3}{5}$ $=5\frac{11}{12}$ $=2\frac{2}{3}$ $=5\frac{1}{6}$

....

....

....

8.1 Constructing perpendicular lines

1 In the space below, make an accurate copy of this diagram by following the steps.

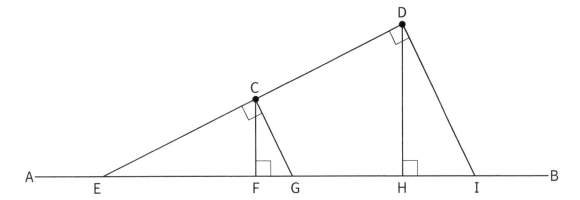

a Construct the perpendicular lines CF and DH.

b Draw the line DC and extend the line to meet AB at the point E.

> You will need to extend your line past D in order to answer part c).

c Construct the perpendicular lines CG and DI.

d Measure and write down the size of angles HDI and CGF.

Angle HDI = ...°   Angle CGF = ...°

e What can you say about triangles HDI and FCG?

....

8.2 Inscribing shapes in circles

In the space below, draw a circle with a radius of 6 cm. Mark the centre of the circle with a dot.

1 a Construct an inscribed square. Measure and write down the side length of the square. . . . .

b Work out the area of:

i the circle . . . .

ii the square . . . .

2 a Draw a circle inside the square so that it touches all the sides of the square.

Measure and write down the radius of the circle. . . . .

b Construct an inscribed equilateral triangle. Measure and write down the base length and the height of the triangle.

Base length = ... Height = ...

c Work out the area of:

i the smaller circle ....

ii the triangle ....

3 What percentage of the area of the biggest circle is the area of the triangle?

....

8.3 Using Pythagoras' theorem

1 The diagram shows a ladder leaning against a wall.

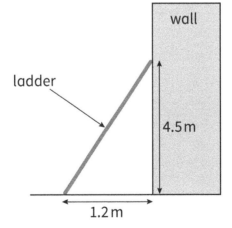

Work out the length of the ladder in m to the nearest cm.

....

....

....

2 The diagram shows two triangles, ABE and CDE.

AB = 10 cm, AE = 8 cm, ED = 3 cm.

The ratio of BE : CE is 3 : 2.

Work out the length of CD.

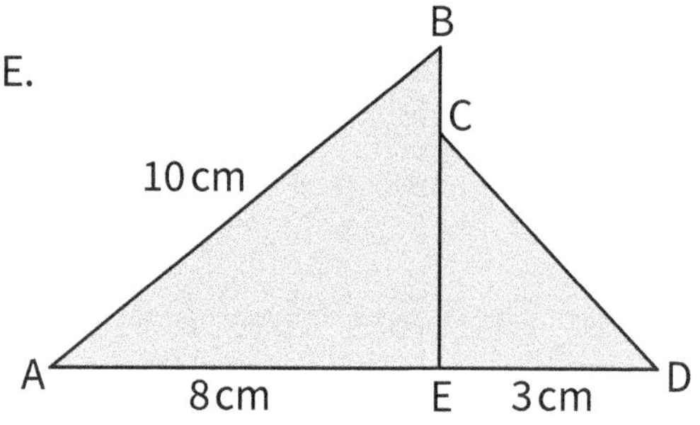

....

....

....

....

....

3 The diagram shows an isosceles trapezium.

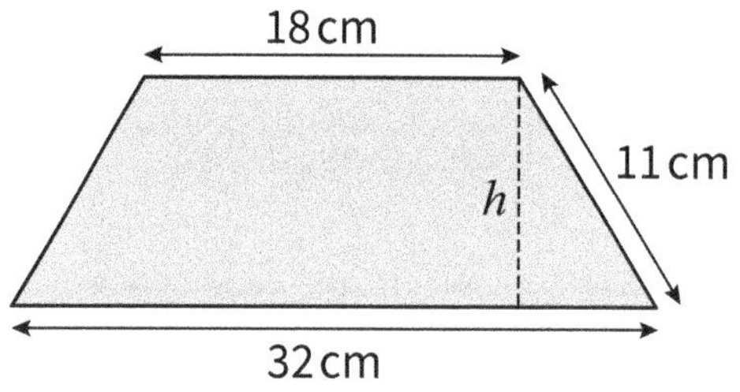

a Work out the height, h, of the trapezium.
Give your answer correct to 2 d.p.

Start by working out this length.

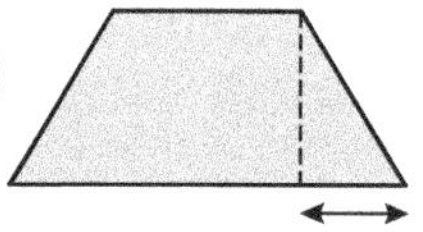

....

....

....

....

b Work out the area of the trapezium. Give your answer correct to 1 d.p.

....

....

Mixed questions

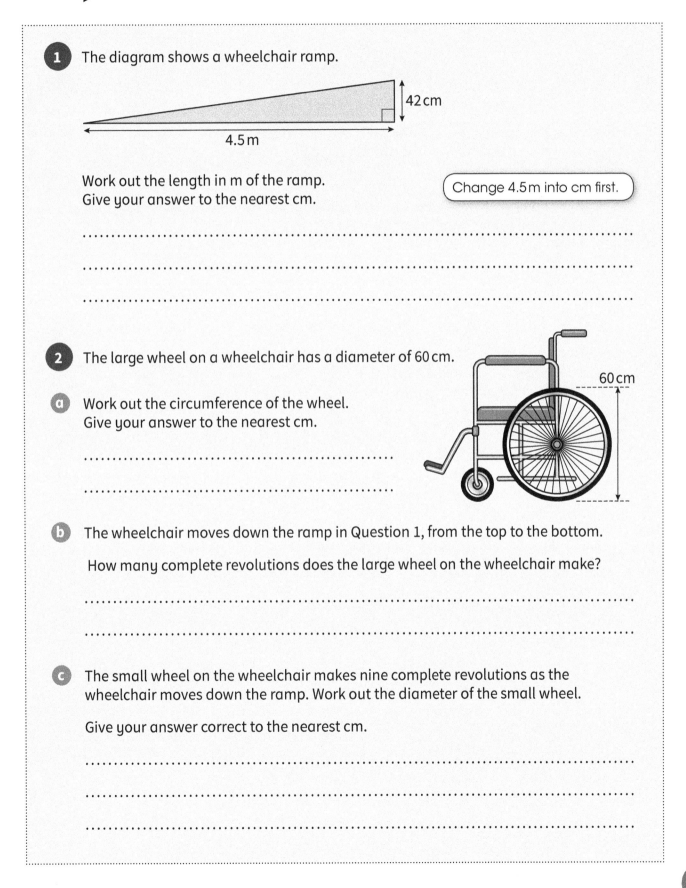

1 The diagram shows a wheelchair ramp.

42 cm

4.5 m

Work out the length in m of the ramp.
Give your answer to the nearest cm.

Change 4.5 m into cm first.

....

....

....

2 The large wheel on a wheelchair has a diameter of 60 cm.

60 cm

a Work out the circumference of the wheel.
Give your answer to the nearest cm.

....

....

b The wheelchair moves down the ramp in Question 1, from the top to the bottom.

How many complete revolutions does the large wheel on the wheelchair make?

....

....

c The small wheel on the wheelchair makes nine complete revolutions as the
wheelchair moves down the ramp. Work out the diameter of the small wheel.

Give your answer correct to the nearest cm.

....

....

....

3   The wheelchair ramp is 1.75 m wide.

The sloping face is a rectangle.

42 cm

4.5 m

1.75 m

Use your answer to Question 1 to help you work out the area of the sloping face of the ramp. Give your answer in m^2 correct to 2 d.p.

....

....

....

....

....

....

....

9 Expressions and formulae

9.1 Simplifying algebraic expressions

1 Complete these division patterns.

a $\dfrac{2^3}{2^5} = \dfrac{2 \times 2 \times 2}{2 \times 2 \times 2 \times 2 \times 2} = \dfrac{1}{2 \times 2} = \dfrac{1}{2^{\square}}$ and $\dfrac{2^3}{2^5} = 2^{3-5} = 2^{-2}$ so $\dfrac{1}{2^{\square}} = 2^{-2}$

b $\dfrac{3^2}{3^6} = \dfrac{3 \times 3}{3 \times 3 \times 3 \times 3 \times 3 \times 3} = \dfrac{1}{3 \times 3 \times 3 \times 3} = \dfrac{1}{3^{\square}}$ and $\dfrac{3^2}{3^6} = 3^{2-6} = 3^{\square}$ so $\dfrac{1}{3^{\square}} = 3^{\square}$

c $\dfrac{x}{x^2} = \dfrac{x}{x \times x} = \dfrac{1}{x} = \dfrac{1}{x^{\square}}$ and $\dfrac{x}{x^2} = x^{1-2} = x^{\square}$ so $\dfrac{1}{x^{\square}} = x^{\square}$

2 Fill in the missing indices in these fractions. The first one has been done for you.

a $4^{-2} = \dfrac{1}{4^2}$

b $5^{-3} = \dfrac{1}{5^{\square}}$

c $8^{-5} = \dfrac{1}{8^{\square}}$

d $x^{-4} = \dfrac{1}{x^{\square}}$

e $y^{-7} = \dfrac{1}{y^{\square}}$

f $z^{-1} = \dfrac{1}{z^{\square}}$

3 Simplify these expressions. Write each one as a negative power and as a fraction. The first one has been started for you.

a $\dfrac{x^5}{x^8} = x^{5-8} = x^{-3} = \dfrac{1}{x^{\square}}$

b $\dfrac{y^3}{y^7}$ ....

c $\dfrac{m^2}{m^{10}}$ ....

d $\dfrac{n}{n^6}$ ....

9.2 Constructing algebraic expressions

1 The graph shows the amount it costs to hire a bicycle.

a How much does it cost to hire a bicycle for:

i 1 day? ......   **ii** 3 days? ......

b How much extra is it per day to hire a bicycle? ......

c There is a standard hire charge, before the amount per day is added on. How much is this charge? ......

> Look at the charge for 0 days.

d Write an expression for the total cost to hire a bike for d days. ....

9.3 Substituting into expressions

1 Here are two expressions that you can use to estimate the mass, in kg, of a child aged between 1 and 5 years old. A is the age, in years, of the child.

Expression ①

$$\frac{5A}{2} + 8$$

Expression ②

$$2(A + 4)$$

a Estimate the mass, in kg, of a 4-year-old child using expression ①.

....

b Estimate the mass, in kg, of a 3-year-old child using expression ②.

....

c Complete the table showing the estimates of the mass of a child using both expressions.

Age (A years)	1	2	3	4	5
Mass using expression ①					
Mass using expression ②					

....

....

....

d Fasil is 3 years old and has a mass of 13.5 kg. Which expression would give the best estimate for his mass? Explain your answer.

....

9.4 Deriving and using formulae

1 Look at these two formulae that are used in science:

$$a = \frac{v - u}{t}$$

$$F = ma$$

a Work out the value of a when $v = 25$, $u = 7$ and $t = 9$.

....

b Work out the value of F when $a = 3$ and $m = 14$.

....

c Work out the value of F when $v = 32$, $u = 12$, $t = 5$ and $m = 30$.

....

....

9.5 Factorising

1 **a** Complete this spider diagram. The four expressions around the edge are all equivalent to the expression in the middle.

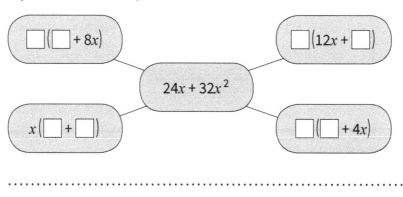

....

....

b Which expression around the edge is the correct fully factorised expression?

....

2 **a** Expand and simplify $4(2x + 3) + 5(x - 4) + 3(5 - 2x)$

....

....

b Factorise your answer to part a).

....

9.6 Adding and subtracting algebraic fractions

You add and subtract fractions by using a common denominator, for example:

$\frac{1}{2} + \frac{1}{3} = \frac{3}{6} + \frac{2}{6} = \frac{5}{6}$

You use the same method with algebraic fractions, for example, $\frac{1}{a} + \frac{1}{b} = \frac{b}{ab} + \frac{a}{ab} = \frac{b+a}{ab}$

1 Use the same method as above to add and subtract these fractions.

a $\frac{1}{x} + \frac{1}{y}$ ....

b $\frac{1}{c} + \frac{1}{d}$ ....

c $\frac{1}{x} - \frac{1}{y}$ ....

d $\frac{2}{a} + \frac{1}{b}$ ....

e $\frac{5}{m} - \frac{2}{n}$ ....

9.7 Expanding the product of two linear expressions

1 Show that $(x+4)(x-3) + x(5-x) = 6(x-2)$

> Start by working with the left-hand side of the equation.

....

....

....

2 **a** Show that $(2x+1)(3x+2) = 6x^2 + 7x + 2$

....

....

b Expand and simplify:

i $(3x + 1)(4x + 5)$

....

ii $(4y + 3)(2y - 5)$

....

Mixed questions

1 **a** Expand and simplify:

i $(x + 6)^2$

....

ii $(x + 5)(x + 7)$

....

What do you notice about your answers to i and ii?

....

2 **a** Expand and simplify:

i $(x + 7)^2$

....

ii $(x + 6)(x + 8)$

....

What do you notice about your answers to i and ii?

....

3 Try some other examples of your own, similar to Questions 1 and 2.
What do you notice?

....

....

....

....

....

....

....

....

....

....

....

....

....

....

....

....

....

....

....

....

10.1 Calculating statistics

Here is a frequency table. It shows the mass, in grams, of 100 packets.

Mass (g)	135	136	137	138	139	140
Frequency	5	17	32	25	18	3

The mean mass is $\dfrac{135 \times 5 + 136 \times 17 + 137 \times 32 + 138 \times 25 + 139 \times 18 + 140 \times 3}{100}$

When you do this with a calculator there are many button presses. It is easy to make a mistake. You can simplify the arithmetic by using an assumed mean.

Suppose the assumed mean is 137.

Mass (g)	Difference from assumed mean, d	Frequency, f	$f \times d$
135	−2	5	−10
136	−1	17	−17
$a = 137$	0	32	0
138	1	25	25
139	2	18	36
140	3	3	9
Total		100	43

The total in the last column is easy to find, even without a calculator.

The mean is $137 + \dfrac{43}{100} = 137.43$

> This is the mean value of d added to the assumed mean a.

1 Complete the table to show that you get the same answer to the question above if you use 138 as the assumed mean.

Mass (g)	Difference, d, from assumed mean	Frequency, f	$f \times d$
135		5	
136		17	
137	–1	32	–32
$a = 138$	0	25	0
139	1	18	18
140		3	
Total		100	

Mean = 138 – . . . . . . = ...

2 Here are the numbers of matches in 50 boxes.

Number of matches	Difference, d, from assumed mean	Frequency, f	$f \times d$
78		5	
79		10	
$a = 80$	0	15	
81		8	
82		8	
83		4	
Total		50	

Use an assumed mean of 80 to find the mean number of matches in a box.

Mean = ...

3 Here are the ages of 40 people.

Age		Frequency	
61		5	
62		8	
63		6	
64		9	
65		12	
Total		40	

Use an assumed mean to find the mean age.

Mean = ...

4 Here are the points scored by 35 people in a competition.

Points		Frequency	
25		10	
26		8	
27		8	
28		6	
29		3	
Total		35	

Use an assumed mean to find the mean number of points.

Mean = ...

5 Here are the times 80 students spend doing their homework.

Time (minutes)		Frequency	
40		6	
50		9	
60		30	
70		17	
80		18	
Total		80	

Use an assumed mean to find the mean time.

Mean = ...

10.2 Using statistics

1 This bar chart shows the ages of 100 people.

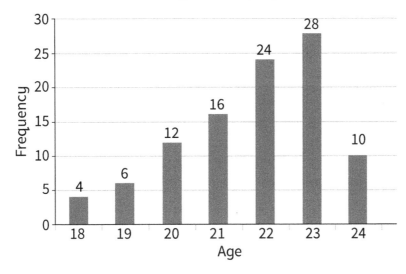

a Find the median age.

Median age = ...

b Find the mean age.

Mean age = ...

c Delete the incorrect word.

The mean is **more/less** than the median.

2 This bar chart shows the ages of 80 people.

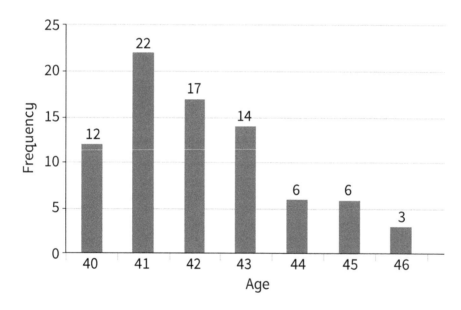

a Find the median age.

Median age = ...

b Find the mean age.

Mean age = ...

c Delete the incorrect word.

The mean is **more/less** than the median.

3 This bar chart shows the test marks of 50 boys and 40 girls.

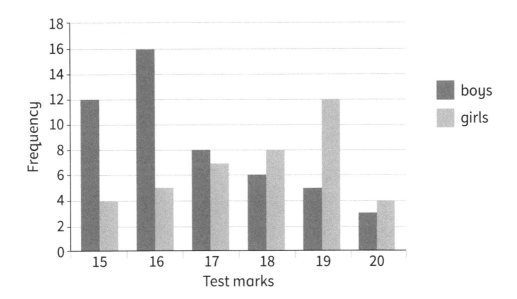

a By looking at the shapes of the graph and without doing any calculations, cross out the incorrect words in these sentences.

The median mark of the girls is **more/less** than the median mark of the boys.

The mean mark of the girls is **more/less** than the median mark of the boys.

For the girls, the median mark is **more/less** than the mean mark.

For the boys, the median mark is **more/less** than the mean mark.

b Work out the median and the mean marks of the girls and of the boys.

You can use the space below for your calculations.

Median of the girls = ...   Median of the boys = ...

Mean of the girls = ...   Mean of the boys = ...

Mixed questions

1 Here are the masses, in kilograms, of 25 children.

Mass (kg)	14	15	16	17	18	19	20
Frequency	2	8	6	3	2	1	3

a Find the median mass.   ...... kg

b Find the modal mass.   ...... kg

c Find the mean mass.   ...... kg

d Find the range.   ...... kg

e There is an error. The correct masses are 2 kg less than the recorded values.

Write down the correct value of:

i the median mass   ...... kg

ii the modal mass   ...... kg

iii the mean mass   ...... kg

iv the range   ...... kg

2 Here are the lengths, in centimetres, of 45 plants.

Length (cm)	9	10	11	12	13	14	15	16
Frequency	6	4	10	7	8	9	0	1

a Find the median length.   ...... cm

b Find the modal length.   ...... cm

c Find the mean length.   ...... cm

d Find the range.   ...... cm

Here are the lengths of the plants two weeks later.

Length (cm)	12	13	14	15	16	17	18	19	20	21
Frequency	3	4	8	8	7	5	3	1	2	4

The gardener wants to find out the change in the average length.

e Which is the best average to use? ......

f Calculate the average you have chosen and state how much it has changed.

....

....

....

3 Here are the ages of the players in two football teams.

Team A: 18 19 21 21 21 23 29 32 33 36 37
Team B: 23 23 24 25 25 26 27 30 30 30 30

Compare the ages of the two teams. Calculate appropriate statistics as part of your answer.

....

....

....

....

11 Percentages

11.1 Using mental methods

It is easy to find 10% of a quantity – you just divide by 10.

By repeated halving, you can find 5% and 2.5%.

Additions and subtractions can give lots more percentages without requiring a calculator. For example:

What is 17.5% of $42.80?

$$10\% = \$4.28$$
$$5\% = \$2.14$$
$$2.5\% = \$1.07$$

Add: 17.5% = $7.49

> Do not use a calculator for these questions.

---

1 Find these percentages of $42.80.

a 15% = ...

b 12.5% = ...

c 22.5% = ...

d 7.5% = ...

e 52.5% = ...

f 1.25% = ...

2 Find the following percentages of $26.40.

a 50% = ...

b 10% = ...

c 5% = ...

d 2.5% = ...

e 12.5% = ...

f 17.5% = ...

g 7.5% = ...

h 57.5% = ...

3 A tax of 15% is added to some prices. Find the tax in these cases.

Price before tax	$14.80	$88	$450	$2.80	$7200
Tax	$2.22				

4 Work out:

a 22.5% of $66 = ...

b 1.25% of $488 = ...

c 27.5% of $24 = ...

d 7.5% of $7600 = ...

A% of B is the same as B% of A.

You can use this fact to change a hard percentage into an easier one. For example:

31.6% of $25 = 25% of $31.60

50% = $15.80 and 25% = $8.90

5 Work out the following percentages. Do not use a calculator for these questions.

a 14.2% of $75 = ...

b 31.3% of $30 = ...

c 88.4% of $25 = ...

d 4.6% of $90 = ...

6 Use any method you like to work out the following percentages.

a 2.5% of $124 = ...

b 13.8% of $60 = ...

c 55% of $93 = ...

d 53.6% of $25 = ...

11.2 Percentage changes

The price of a car increases from $12 490 to $12 840.

You can work out the percentage change like this:

$$\frac{\text{new price}}{\text{old price}} = \frac{12840}{12490} = 1.028 = 102.8\%$$

The calculator answer is rounded to 3 d.p.

The old price was 100%, so the increase is 2.8%.

1 Work out the percentage increase each time.

a The price of a computer increases from $675 to $699.

Increase = ... %

b The price of a flight increases from $329 to $384.

Increase = ... %

c The price of a holiday increases from $1199 to $1349.

Increase = ... %

d The rent of an apartment increases from $525 to $580.

Increase = ... %

(e) The population of a country increases from 17.41 million to 29.65 million.

Increase = ... %

(f) The mass of a young child increases from 4.15 kg to 9.28 kg.

Increase = ... %

The method also works for percentage decreases.

Suppose the price of the car in the last example is reduced from $12 840 to $12 490.

$$\frac{\text{new price}}{\text{old price}} = \frac{12490}{12840} = 0.973 = 97.3\%.$$

The decrease from 100% is 2.7%.

(2) Work out the percentage decrease each time.

(a) The price of a computer decreases from $699 to $675.

Decrease = ... %

(b) The price of a coat decreases from $179 to $129.

Decrease = ... %

(c) The price of a table decreases from $485 to $269.

Decrease = ... %

(d) The record time for a race reduces from 56.3 s to 49.1 s.

Decrease = ... %

(e) The mass of a man reduces from 92.6 kg to 77.2 kg.

Decrease = ... %

(f) The population of a town reduces from 29 452 to 12 817.

Decrease = ... %

3 Find the percentage change in each case. Say if it is an increase or a decrease.

a A price changes from $3545 to $4280. ....

b A mass changes from 29.3 kg to 17.6 kg. ....

c An area changes from 3721 km² to 892 km². ....

d A population changes from 34.5 million to 43.1 million. ....

4 The height of a tree increases by 0.5 m each year. Complete the table and find the percentage change from one year to the next each time.

Year	2016	2017	2018	2019	2020
Height	2.5 m	3.0 m	3.5 m		
Annual percentage change	20%				

....

....

Mixed questions

1 Without using a calculator, find:

a 1.25% of $4280 = ...

b 17.5% of $644 ......

c 81.6% of $25 = ...

d 22% of $22 ......

2 There are 324 men and 259 women in a college.

218 of the men are studying engineering.

The percentage of women studying engineering is the same as the percentage of men.

How many women are studying engineering?

.... women

3 The number of flights per day increases from 125 to 180.

a Find the percentage increase. ......%

b The number of flights increases by the same percentage again.

Work out the number of flights per day now. ......

4 Maha looks at her pay for this month.

Payslip			
Employee: _____Maha_____			
Earnings	**Amount**	**Deductions**	**Amount**
Total pay	$1280.00		
		Deductions for income tax	$294.40
Money received	$985.60		

Maha does this calculation. $\frac{294.40}{985.60} \times 100 = 29.87$

She says: 'I have paid nearly 30% of my pay in income tax.'

a What mistake has Maha made?

....

....

b Work out the correct percentage for Maha. . . . . . . %

c Here are details of Razi's pay.

Payslip			
Employee: Razi			
Earnings	**Amount**	**Deductions**	**Amount**
Total pay	$930.00		
		Deductions for income tax	$195.30
Money received	$734.70		

Compare the tax paid by Razi and Maha.

. . . .

. . . .

5 The cost of fuel is $4.80 a litre. This includes 25% tax.

Jake says that the tax is 25% of $4.80 = $1.20.

a Explain why Jake is incorrect.

. . . .

. . . .

b Show that the tax is actually $0.96.

. . . .

. . . .

12 Tessellations, transformations and loci

12.1 Tessellating shapes

1 Hassan uses these tiles to make a tessellation. The first tile is a parallelogram and the second tile is a rhombus.

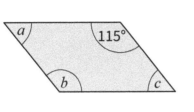
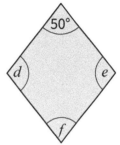

a Work out the sizes of the angles marked with letters.

....

....

....

b Draw a sketch to show how these tiles will tessellate together. Include at least four of each tile in your sketch.

2 Draw a tessellation for each part on the dotted paper, using the shapes given.

Draw at least five more shapes for each part.

a

b

c

d

12.2 Solving transformation problems

1 Look at this grid.

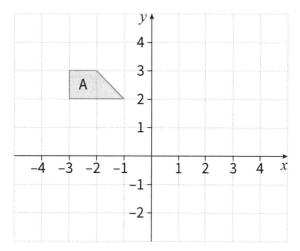

a Translate shape A using the vector $\begin{pmatrix} 2 \\ -4 \end{pmatrix}$, label it B.

b Translate shape B using the vector $\begin{pmatrix} 2 \\ 3 \end{pmatrix}$, label it C.

c What is the vector that translates shape A directly to shape C? ......

What do you notice about your answer and the vectors in parts a) and b)?

....

d Fill in the missing numbers in these statements.

i Translating a shape $\begin{pmatrix} 1 \\ 3 \end{pmatrix}$ and then $\begin{pmatrix} 5 \\ 2 \end{pmatrix}$ is the same as the single vector $\begin{pmatrix} \\ \end{pmatrix}$

ii Translating a shape $\begin{pmatrix} -2 \\ 6 \end{pmatrix}$ and then $\begin{pmatrix} -3 \\ -4 \end{pmatrix}$ is the same as the single vector $\begin{pmatrix} \\ \end{pmatrix}$

12.3 Transforming shapes

1 In the diagram, shape A has been reflected and then translated to give shape B.

Describe a possible reflection and translation that will transform shape A to shape B.

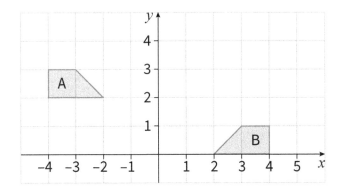

....

....

2 In the diagram, shape C has been reflected and then rotated to give shape D.

Describe a possible reflection and rotation that will transform shape C to shape D.

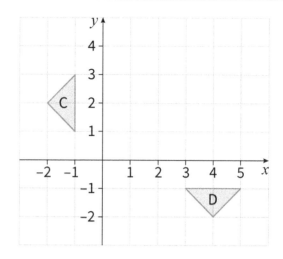

....

....

12.4 Enlarging shapes

You can enlarge a shape using a scale factor which is a fraction.

When the fraction is less than 1, the enlarged shape will be smaller than the shape you started with.

1 Complete the enlargement of triangle ABC using a scale factor of $\frac{1}{2}$ and centre of enlargement O.

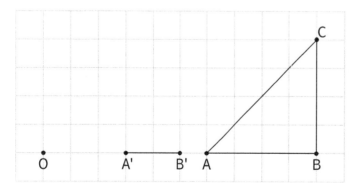

The distance from O to A is 6 squares, so the distance from O to A' is $\frac{1}{2}$ of 6 = 3 squares.
The distance from A to B is 4 squares, so the distance from A' to B' is $\frac{1}{2}$ of 4 = 2 squares.

2 Enlarge shape ABCD using a scale factor of $\frac{1}{3}$ and centre of enlargement O.

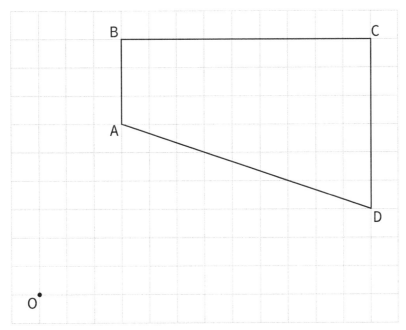

12.5 Drawing a locus

1 The map shows three radio masts, A, B and C. The map has a scale of 1 cm represents 15 km.

A
•

B
•

•
C

Mast A transmits a signal to a distance of 45 km.

Mast B transmits a signal to a distance of 60 km.

Mast C transmits a signal to a distance of 75 km.

a Draw the locus of points that are exactly:

i 45 km from A   **ii** 60 km from B   **iii** 75 km from C

b Shade the area in which you can get a signal from all three masts at the same time.

Mixed questions

1 The diagram shows shape X. Draw the image of X after a reflection in the line $x = -2$, followed by a rotation of 90° clockwise about the point $(-1, 0)$, followed by a translation using the vector $\begin{pmatrix} 4 \\ 3 \end{pmatrix}$.

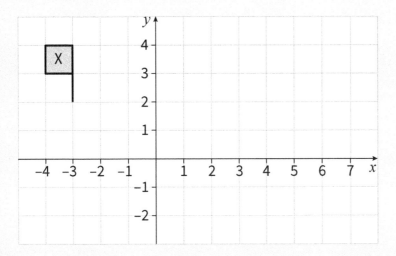

2 On the diagram below, draw the locus of the points that are exactly 15 mm from the line.

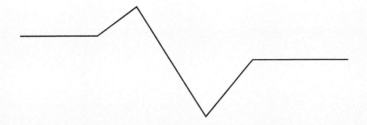

13 Equations and inequalities

13.1 Solving linear equations

Here is an equation that involves division:

$$\frac{2x}{3} + 5 = 13$$

$\frac{2x}{3}$ means $2 \times x \div 3$

To solve this you must multiply by 3. Here are two methods:

First method		Second method	
	$\frac{2x}{3} + 5 = 13$		$\frac{2x}{3} + 5 = 13$
Subtract 5	$\frac{2x}{3} = 8$	Multiply by 3	$2x + 15 = 39$
Multiply by 3	$2x = 24$	Subtract 15	$2x = 24$
Divide by 2	$x = 12$	Divide by 2	$x = 12$

You can use either method.

1. Solve these equations.

a) $\frac{x}{4} - 6 = 3$ ....

b) $\frac{x}{5} + 4 = 12$ ....

c) $\frac{2x}{3} - 2 = 8$ ....

d) $\frac{3x}{2} + 6 = 24$ ....

e) $\frac{2x}{5} - 1 = 7$ ....

f) $\frac{5x}{3} + 4 = 19$ ....

Here is a more complicated equation:

$$\frac{2x}{3} + \frac{x}{2} = 7$$

Here are two methods of solving the equation:

First method		Second method	
	$\frac{2x}{3} + \frac{x}{2} = 7$		$\frac{2x}{3} + \frac{x}{2} = 7$
Multiply by 3	$2x + \frac{3x}{2} = 21$	Multiply by 6	$4x + 3x = 42$
Multiply by 2	$4x + 3x = 42$	Add terms	$7x = 42$
Add terms	$7x = 42$	Divide by 6	$x = 7$
Divide by 6	$x = 7$		

In the first method you multiply by 2 and 3 separately.

Because 2 × 3 = 6, you can also use the second method and multiply by 6.

You can use either method.

2 Solve these equations.

a $\frac{x}{2} + x = 18$ ....

b $\frac{2x}{3} + 2x = 16$ ....

....

....

c $\frac{x}{3} + \frac{x}{2} = 10$ ....

d $\frac{x}{2} - \frac{x}{3} = 4$ ....

....

....

e $2x = \frac{x}{2} + 12$ ....

f $\frac{2x}{3} + \frac{x}{4} = 22$ ....

....

....

3 Solve these equations.

a $\dfrac{x-3}{4} = 5$ ....

....

b $\dfrac{2x+1}{3} = 8$ ....

....

c $\dfrac{x-4}{2} = \dfrac{x}{4}$ ....

....

d $\dfrac{x-3}{3} = \dfrac{x+7}{4}$ ....

....

13.2 Trial and improvement

1 Here is an equation: $x^3 + x = 12$.

a Fill in the values in this table.

x	$x^3 + x$
2	10
2.1	
2.2	
2.14	
2.15	

b Complete this sentence.

The solution is between ...... and ......

2 You can solve the equation $x^3 + x = 12$ by trial and improvement.

Here is a different method:

Rewrite the equation $\quad x^3 = 12 - x$

$$x = \sqrt[3]{12 - x}$$

You know the solution is close to 2. Write $x_1 = 2$.

Then $x_2 = \sqrt[3]{12 - x_1} = \sqrt[3]{12 - 2} = \sqrt[3]{10} = 2.154434\ldots$

a Find the value of $x_2 = \sqrt[3]{10}$ on your calculator.

> Do not round off the value of x_2 when you calculate x_3. Write down all the digits of your calculator answer.

b Work out the value of $x_3 = \sqrt[3]{12 - x_2}$

$x_3 = \ldots\ldots\ldots\ldots\ldots\ldots\ldots\ldots$

c Work out the value of $x_4 = \sqrt[3]{12 - x_3}$

Write down all the digits of your calculator answer.

$x_4 = \ldots\ldots\ldots\ldots\ldots\ldots\ldots\ldots$

d Work out the value of $x_5 = \sqrt[3]{12 - x_4}$

Write down all the digits of your calculator answer.

$x_5 = \ldots\ldots\ldots\ldots\ldots\ldots\ldots\ldots$

e What do you notice about the values of $x_1, x_2, x_3, \ldots$

$\ldots\ldots\ldots\ldots\ldots\ldots\ldots\ldots\ldots\ldots\ldots\ldots\ldots\ldots\ldots\ldots\ldots\ldots\ldots\ldots\ldots\ldots\ldots\ldots\ldots\ldots\ldots\ldots\ldots\ldots$

f Use the value you have to write down the solution of the equation $x^3 + x = 12$ correct to 3 decimal places. $\quad x = \ldots\ldots$

3 Here is an equation: $x^3 + x = 40$.

a Show that the solution is larger than 3.

....

b Show that the equation can be written as $x = \sqrt[3]{40 - x}$

....

c Start with $x_1 = 3$ and find the next terms. Give a full calculator answer.

$x_2 = $ ....

$x_3 = $ ....

$x_4 = $ ....

$x_5 = $ ....

d Write down the solution of the equation $x^3 + x = 40$ correct to 4 d.p.

4 Use this method to solve the equation $x^3 + x = 150$.

Show your method. Give your answer correct to 5 d.p.

....

....

....

....

....

.... $x = $ ......

Mixed questions

1 Solve the equation $3x - 12 = x + 15$.

....

$x = $ ......

2 Solve the equation $2(x + 5) = 5(x - 6)$.

....

$x = \ldots\ldots$

3 $x + y = 21$ and $x - y = 5$

Find the value of $2x + 3y$.

....

....

....

$x = \ldots\ldots$ and $y = \ldots\ldots$

4 Sasha thinks of four consecutive whole numbers.

a If the smallest number is N, write down the other three numbers in terms of N.

....

b Sasha says: 'The sum of four numbers is 654.'

Write down an equation using N.

....

c Solve the equation to find the smallest number.

....

$N = \ldots\ldots$

5 Xavier buys two items. He receives $2.26 change from $40.

The difference between the prices of the two items is $9.24.

Find the cost of each item.

....

$\ldots\ldots$ and $\ldots\ldots$

6 This is a graph of $y = x + \dfrac{1}{x}$ $x > 0$

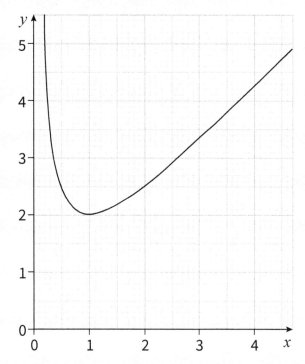

a How does the graph show that the equation $x + \dfrac{1}{x} = 3$ has two solutions?

....

b Use the graph to estimate the larger of the two solutions. . . . . . .

c Use trial and improvement to find the larger solution correct to 2 d.p.

Put your trials in the table.

x	$x + \dfrac{1}{x}$

$x =$ . . . . . . to 2 d.p.

14 Ratio and proportion

14.1 Comparing and using ratios

1 The height and width of a rectangular screen can be written in the ratio height : width. This is called the aspect ratio.

width

height

Write each of these aspect ratios as unit ratios in the form $1 : n$.

a

4

Regular TV screen

3

....

....

b

16

Widescreen TV

9

....

....

c

12

Calculator screen

5

....

....

d

7

Cinema screen

3

....

....

e Which of the screens above has the greatest aspect ratio? Explain your answer.

....

....

2 The power-to-weight ratio of a car is a measure of the performance of the car engine.

A high power-to-weight ratio means that a car will perform well.

a Use a calculator to work out the power-to-weight ratio for each of these cars.

Complete the table. Write your answer as a unit ratio in the form $n : 1$.

Round n to the nearest whole number. The first one has been done for you.

Car	Power (kW)	Weight (tonne)	Power : weight (unit ratio)
Ford model T (1908)	15	0.540	28 : 1
Mini 1275GT (1969)	57	0.686	
Ferrari Testarossa (1984)	291	1.506	
Land Rover Defender (1990)	90	1.837	
Ariel Atom 3S (2014)	272	0.639	
Koenigsegg One (2015)	1000	1.310	

$$15 : 0.54 = \frac{15}{0.54} : 1$$

$$15 \div 0.54 = 27.7\ldots$$

....

....

....

....

....

....

b Which car performs the best? Explain your answer.

....

....

3 All three pictures have their sides in the same ratio.

4 cm

6 cm

6 cm

☐ cm

☐ cm

15 cm

Work out the missing lengths.

....

....

14.2 Solving problems

1 Mia travels from the USA to Mexico to France and then back to the USA.

The table shows some currency exchange rates.

Currency exchange rates		
$1 = 18.5 pesos	1 peso = €0.05	€1 = $1.10

Before leaving the USA, Mia changes $1500 into Mexican pesos. In Mexico she spends 8140 pesos. She changes the remainder of her pesos into euros (€). While in France she spends €810.50.

She changes the remainder of her euros back into US dollars.

How many dollars does she have left?

....

....

....

....

2 These are some ratios that are used to estimate the height of a person.

Hand span : height = 1 : 10

Width of shoulders : height = 1 : 4

Distance from elbow to tip of hand : height = 1 : 5

Distance from elbow to armpit : height = 1 : 8

Hassan has a hand span of 18.7 cm. The width of Joe's shoulders is 45 cm.

The distance from Carlos's elbow to the tip of his hand is 38 cm.

The distance from Ismail's elbow to his armpit is 23 cm.

Estimate the height of each man. Write their names in order of height from the shortest to the tallest.

....

....

....

....

....

....

....

....

....

....

....

....

....

....

Mixed questions

1 At a riding stables, riders are put in groups according to their ability.

The ability groups are walking (W), trotting (T) or cantering (C).

This booking sheet shows the riders and their ability for one ride.

Name of horse	Name of rider	Ability		Name of horse	Name of rider	Ability
Summer	I Read	W		Phantom	M Cowpe	W
Apache	G Jebson	T		Eagle	B Shen	C
Bob	F Khan	W		Merlin	L Read	C
Teddy	C Balewa	C		Harry	S Anderson	T
Ironman	A Zhou	C		Silver	B Balewa	T
Cobweb	A Read	C		Flanagan	L Balewa	T
Colorado	T Khan	W		Rio	B Anderson	T
Andaluz	G Balewa	W		Melody	J Read	C
Georgio	A Jebson	T		Aswan	A Khan	W
Megan	E Cowpe	W		Shiraz	J Garcia	T
Speckles	R Tang	C		Havana	J Cowpe	T
Bee	A Diaz	C		Boudica	S Hoyle	C

a How many riders are there of each ability?

...... walking   ...... trotting   ...... cantering

b The table shows the maximum ratios of staff : riders that the stables use.

It also shows the maximum number of riders that they will have in each group.

Ability	Staff : riders	Maximum number of riders per group
Walking	1 : 3	9
Trotting	1 : 2	6
Cantering	1 : 5	5

> For example, when there are 15 walking, you could have one group of 9 with 3 staff and one group of 6 with 2 staff.

Decide how many groups of each ability are needed and how many riders are in each group.

Work out the number of staff needed for each group.

What is the total number of staff needed for this ride?

....

....

....

....

....

....

....

....

....

....

....

....

....

15 Area, perimeter and volume

15.1 Converting units of area and volume

1 Convert:

a $2\,m^2$ to mm^2.

....

b $0.054\,m^2$ to mm^2.

....

c $78\,000\,000\,mm^2$ to m^2.

....

d $350\,000\,mm^2$ to m^2.

....

2 Dakarai pours 0.6 litres of milk into a square-based tin.

15 mm →

The milk reaches a height of 15 mm in the tin.

What is the side length of the tin?

....

....

....

....

3 A tap drips every second into a rectangular sink.

The diagram shows the dimensions of the sink.

Four drips have a volume of 1 ml.

With the plug in, how long would it take the sink to overflow?

Give your answer in hours, minutes and seconds.

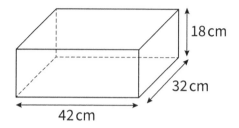

18 cm

32 cm

42 cm

....

....

....

....

 ## 15.2 Using hectares

1 In some countries areas of land are measured in hectares (ha) or square kilometres (km^2).

In other countries, areas of land are measure in acres (ac) or square miles (mi^2).

Here are some conversions.

$1\,km^2 = 100\,ha$ $1\,mi^2 = 2.59\,km^2$ $1\,mi^2 = 640\,ac$

The table shows the areas of four islands in the world.

Island	kilometres^2	hectares	miles^2	acres
Kyushu	37437			
Sardinia		2 394 900		
Spitsbergen			15051	
Timor				7 022 080

a Complete the table. Use the space below for your workings.

....

....

....

....

....

....

....

....

b Write the islands in order of size from the largest to the smallest.

....

....

15.3 **Solving circle problems**

1 The diagram shows a square plastic tray with holes for holding cups.

What is the area of the plastic?

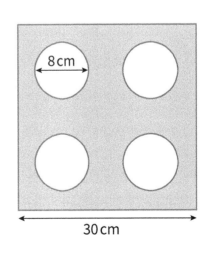

....

....

....

2   The diagram shows an athletics track. The radius of the inner semicircle at each end is 36.8 m. The length of the straight section is 84.39 m.

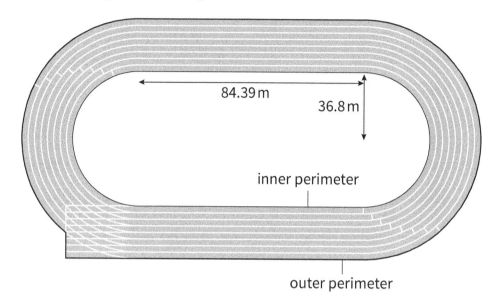

84.39 m

36.8 m

inner perimeter

outer perimeter

a   Work out the length of the inner perimeter of the track.

Give your answer correct to the nearest metre.

....

....

....

b   The width of each lane is 1.22 m. There are eight lanes.

Work out the radius of the outer semicircle at each end of the track.

....

....

c   Work out the length of the outer perimeter of the track.

Give your answer correct to 2 d.p.

....

....

....

15.4 Calculating with prisms and cylinders

1 The diagram shows a bar of gold.

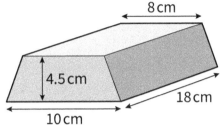

a Work out the volume of gold in the bar.

....

....

b The density of gold is 19 g/cm^3.

Work out the mass of the gold bar in grams.

> Each cubic centimetre of gold has a mass of 19 g.

....

....

c The value of gold varies. Alicia bought this bar of gold when the value of gold was $35 per gram. She sold it when the value of gold was $42 per gram.

How much money did Alicia make?

....

....

....

2 A shop sells hot chocolate powder in three different sized cylindrical tins.

7 cm

$2.31

14 cm

9 cm

$5.39

17 cm

12 cm

$12.59

25 cm

Which tin gives the best value for money?

Work out the price per cm³ for each tin.

....

....

....

....

....

....

....

....

....

....

....

....

....

....

....

....

Mixed questions

1 These prisms all have the same volume. Work out the missing lengths, h, x and y.

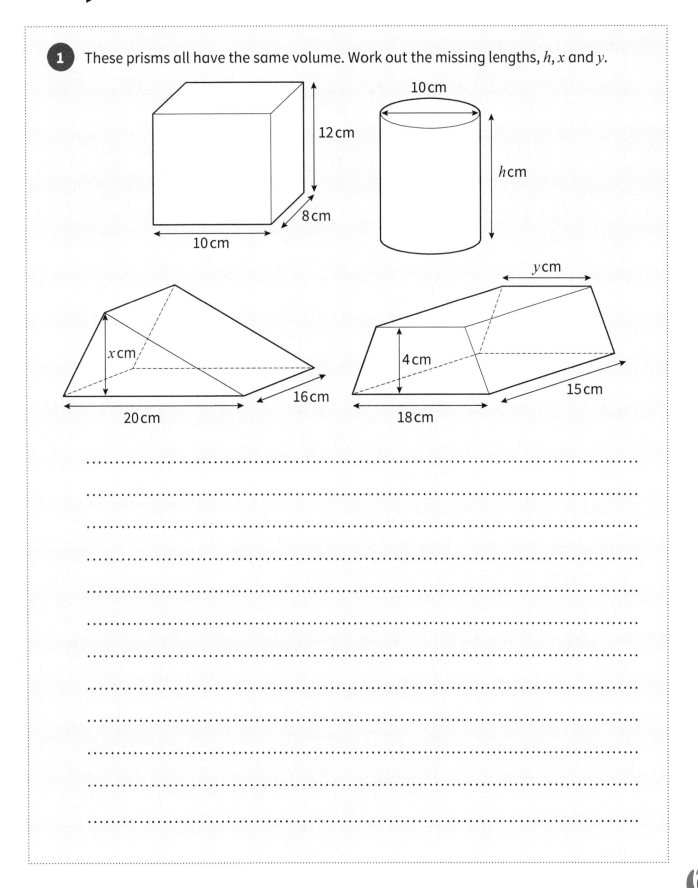

....

....

....

....

....

....

....

....

....

....

....

....

16.1 Sample space diagrams

Here are two fair spinners. Each has four sections, numbered 1 to 4.

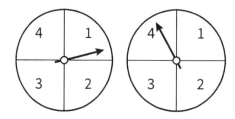

Here is the sample space diagram:

The probability that both numbers are even is $\frac{4}{16} = \frac{1}{4}$.

Suppose you are told that at least one of the numbers is even.

Now the sample space diagram is different. It looks like this:

Now the probability that both numbers are even is $\frac{4}{12} = \frac{1}{3}$.

1 Here are two fair spinners:

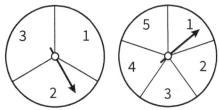

Here is the sample space diagram:

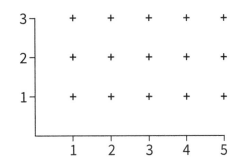

a Find the probability that both numbers are even.   . . . .

b Find the probability that both numbers are odd.   . . . .

c Suppose that at least one number is even.

   i Draw the new sample space diagram.

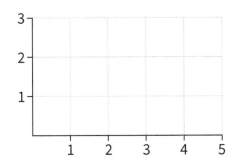

  ii Find the probability that both numbers are even.   . . . .

d Suppose that at least one number is odd.

i Draw the new sample space diagram.

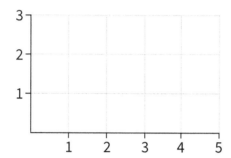

ii Find the probability that both numbers are odd. . . . .

2 Here are two fair spinners:

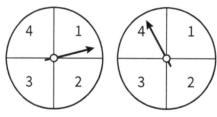

a Find the probability that the total is:

i 6 . . . .   **ii** at least 6 . . . .

b Suppose the total is at least 4.

Draw the sample space diagram.

c If the total is at least 4, find the probability that it is:

i 6 . . . .   **ii** at least 6 . . . .

3 Here are two fair spinners:

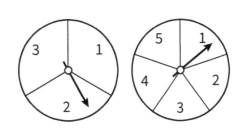

The total score is less than 6.

a Draw a sample space diagram.

b If the total is less than 6, find the probability that:

   i the total is 3 or less ....

   ii both numbers are odd ....

4 Two six-sided dice numbered 1–6 are thrown. At least one dice shows an even number.

a Draw the sample space diagram.

b Find the probability of each of these outcomes.

   i Two even numbers ....

   ii Two odd numbers ....

   iii A total of 8 or more ....

   iv Both dice show the same number ....

16.2 Using relative frequency

Here are the first 100 decimal places of the number π:

$\pi = 3.$ 14159 26535 89793 23846 26433 83279 50288 41971 69399 37510

        58209 74944 59230 78164 06286 20899 86280 34825 34211 70679

Are all the digits equally likely or do some occur more than others?

Digit	10	20	30	40	50	60	70	80	90	100
0	0	0								
1	2	2	2	4	5	5	6	6	6	8
2	1	2								
3	1	3								
4	1	2								
5	3	3								
6	1	2								
7	0	1								
8	0	2								
9	1	3								

The table shows how often each digit occurs in the first 10 places, then the first 20, then the first 30, and so on.

1 The relative frequency of 1 in the first 10 digits is $\frac{2}{10} = 0.2$.

The relative frequency of 1 in the first 20 digits is $\frac{2}{20} = 0.1$.

The relative frequency of 1 in the first 30 digits is $\frac{2}{30} = 0.067$.

a Complete this table of relative frequencies for the digit 1.

Number of digits	10	20	30	40	50	60	70	80	90	100
Relative frequency	0.2	0.1	0.067							

b Plot the relative frequencies on this graph. Join the points with line segments.

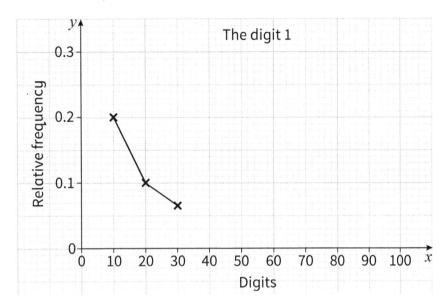

c If the digits are random, write down the probability that a particular digit is a 1. ......

d On the graph, draw a horizontal line from the *y*-axis through the probability in part c).

e Choose a different digit and complete the row in the table at the start of this section for that digit.

f Fill in this table of relative frequencies for your digit.

Number of digits	10	20	30	40	50	60	70	80	90	100
Relative frequency										

g Draw a graph to show the changing relative frequencies for your digit.

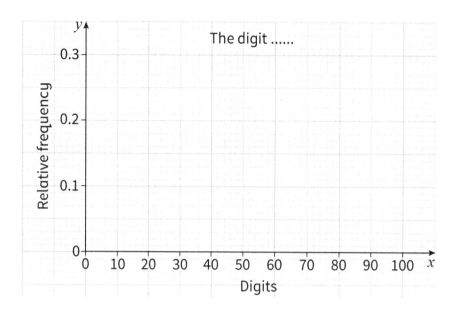

h Look at any graphs that other students have drawn for other digits. Compare them with the two graphs you have drawn. Are they similar? In what way?

....

....

i This table shows the relative frequencies of the digits in the first 1000 places of π.

Digits	0	1	2	3	4	5	6	7	8	9
Relative frequency	0.093	0.116	0.103	0.103	0.093	0.097	0.094	0.095	0.101	0.105

Compare these with any relative frequencies you have for 100 digits of π.

....

....

Mixed questions

1 A football team can win, draw or lose.

The manager says this about the team's next match:

'The probability that we will win is twice the probability that we will draw.

The probability that we will draw is twice the probability that we will lose.'

Find the probability that the team will win.

....

2 The numbers on a six-sided dice are 1, 1, 2, 2, 2 and 3.

The dice is thrown twice. Find the probability of throwing:

a 1 on both dice . . . . . .   **b** a total of 4 . . . . . .

3 This table shows the record of a plane on 40 flights between two cities.

On time	Late by less than 30 minutes	Late by 30 minutes or more	Total
24	10	6	40

a Estimate the probability that the plane will be late by 30 minutes or more.

....

b If the plane is late, find the probability that it is more than 30 minutes late.

....

4 In the number π, the following sequence of digits appears ...... 55252555225......

Tick (✓) all the true statements in the following list.

a The probability that the next digit is 5 is less than 0.1. ......

b The probability that the next digit is 5 is more than 0.1. ......

c The probability that the next digit is 2 is less than 0.1. ......

d The probability that the next digit is 2 is more than 0.1. ......

e The probability that the next digit is 0 is 0.1. ......

5 The table shows the number of people who passed or failed a driving test one week.

	Pass	**Fail**	**Total**
Men	63	22	85
Women	42	10	52
Total	105	32	137

One of the people is selected at random to fill in a questionnaire.

Estimate the probability that the person is:

a a man ......

b a woman who failed the test ......

c a person who passed the test ......

The person who was selected at random was a man.

d Find the probability that he failed the test. ......

17 Bearings and scale drawings

Using bearings

1   The diagram shows three points: A, B and C.

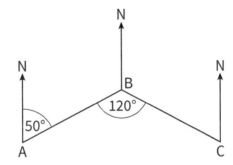

The diagram is not drawn accurately.

a   Write down the bearing of B from A.

   ....

b   Work out the bearing of A from B.

   ....

c   Work out the bearing of C from B.

   ....

d   Work out the bearing of B from C.

   ....

2 The diagram shows a regular hexagon, ABCDEF.

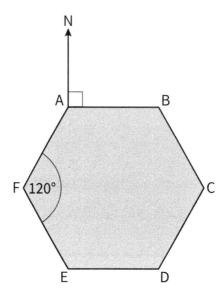

All the internal angles are 120°.

a Write down the bearing to get from A to B.

....

b Work out the bearings to get from:

i B to C ....

ii C to D ....

iii D to E ....

iv E to F ....

v F to A ....

17.2 Making scale drawings

1 The sketch shows an equilateral triangle ABC of side length 5 cm.

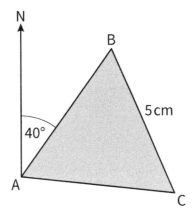

The bearing of B from A is 040°.

a Work out the bearing of C from B.

....

b Work out the bearing of A from C.

....

c Make an accurate copy of the sketch.

2 A boat sails 120 km from a port on a bearing of 075°. It then changes direction and sails 100 km on a bearing of 145°. Finally it sails 150 km on a bearing of 260°.

a Draw an accurate diagram of this journey. Use a scale of 1 cm = 20 km.

N

Port

b How far and on what bearing must the boat sail to return to port?

....

Mixed questions

1 In an orienteering competition you have a map and a compass. You have to visit every marker on the map by using a bearing from one marker to the next. You can visit the markers in any order. The winner is the quickest person to finish.

The map shows an orienteering course. The scale of the map is 1 : 20 000.

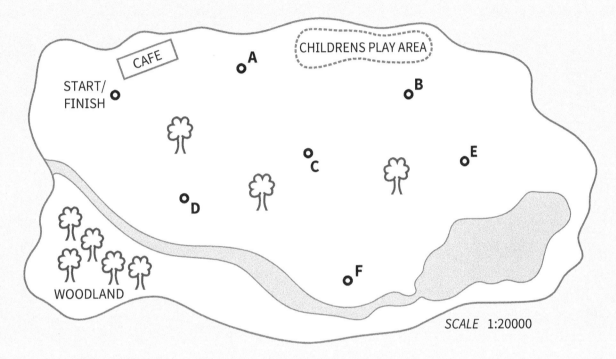

Choose a route from the start to the finish that visits every marker. The markers are labelled A to F.

Complete the table below. What is the total distance on the ground of your route?

....

From	To	Bearing	Distance on map (cm)	Distance on ground (m)
Start				
	Finish			

18 Graphs

18.1 Gradient of a graph

The two axes on a graph do not always have the same scale.

Look at this graph:

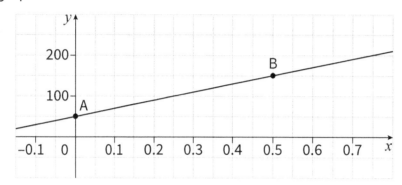

Use the coordinates of A (0, 50) and B (0.5, 150) to find the gradient.

$$\text{Gradient} = \frac{150 - 50}{0.5 - 0} = 200$$

1 Find the gradient of these lines.

a

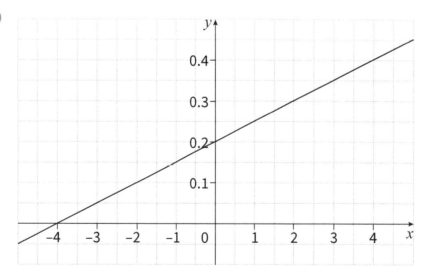

Gradient = ...

b

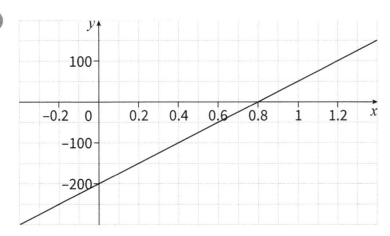

Gradient = ...

c

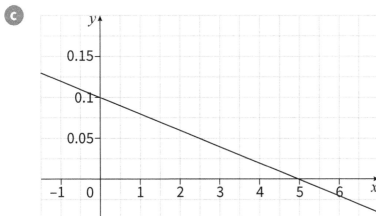

Gradient = ...

d

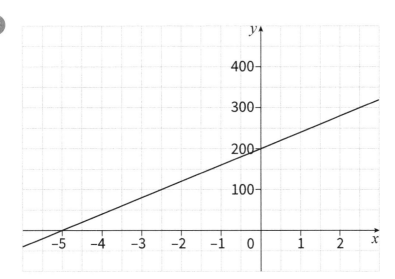

Gradient = ...

e

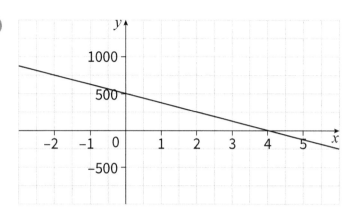

Gradient = ...

f

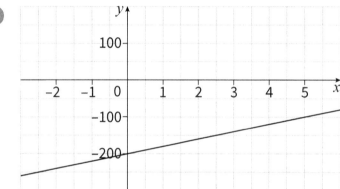

Gradient = ...

2 These three lines all go through (10, 1)

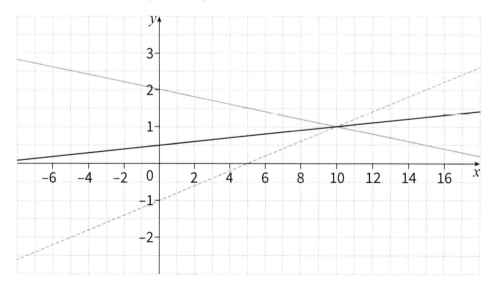

Find their gradients.

....

18.2 The graph of $y = mx + c$

A straight line passes through $(10, 20)$ and $(15, 50)$.

You can use this fact to find the equation of the line.

The gradient is $\dfrac{50 - 20}{15 - 10} = 6$

The equation of the line is $y = 6x + c$.

To find c, put the coordinates of one point $(10, 20)$ in this equation:

$$20 = 6 \times 10 + c$$

Multiply $\quad\quad 20 = 60 + c$

Subtract 60 $\quad\quad c = -40$

> You could use $(15, 50)$ instead and you would get the same answer.

The equation of the line is $y = 6x - 40$.

---

1 Find the equation of the straight line through $(5, 30)$ and $(8, 42)$.

....

....

2 Find the equation of the straight line through $(4, 8)$ and $(6, 9)$.

....

....

3 Find the equation of the straight line through $(10, 8)$ and $(14, 16)$.

....

....

4 Find the equation of the straight line through $(6, 2)$ and $(7, 0)$.

....

....

5 Find the equation of the straight line through (–4, 10) and (6, 12).

....

....

6 Find the equation of the straight line through (3, 100) and (5, 180).

....

....

7 Find the equation of the straight line through (20, –10) and (30, –9).

....

....

8 Find the equation of the straight line through (–12, 6) and (–10, 12).

....

....

18.3 Direct proportion

This table gives the exchange rates for some currencies.

Currency	One US dollar
Euro	0.8906
Hong Kong dollar	7.756
Singapore dollar	1.355
Indian rupee	66.06

For example, 1 US dollar is worth 0.8906 euros.

This means that 260 US dollars are worth 260 × 0.8906 = 231.56 euros and 260 euros are worth 260 ÷ 0.8906 = 291.94 US dollars.

1 **a** Convert 350 US dollars into Hong Kong dollars. ......

b Convert 820 Hong Kong dollars into US dollars. ......

2 **a** Convert 720 US dollars into Singapore dollars. ......

b Convert 2000 Singapore dollars into US dollars. ......

3 **a** Convert 140 US dollars into Indian rupees. ......

b Convert 5400 Indian rupees into US dollars. ......

4 Convert 250 euros into Hong Kong dollars.

....

5 Convert 350 Singapore dollars into Indian rupees.

....

6 Convert 9800 Indian rupees into euros.

....

Mixed questions

1 The gradient of a straight line is 3 and it passes through (6, 8).

Find the equation of the line.

....

....

2 These four straight lines form a square.

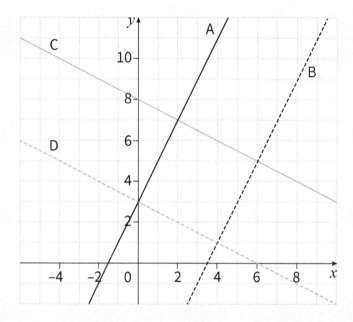

Work out the equation of each of the lines.

....

....

....

A...........   B...........   C...........   D...........

3 23.2 litres of petrol costs $33.64.

a Find the cost of 15.2 litres of petrol. $ . . . . . .

b A formula for the cost, y dollars, of x litres of petrol is $y = mx$.

Find the value of the number m. m = ...

c Draw a graph to show the relationship between litres and cost.

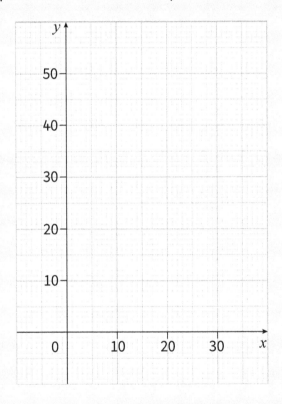

d Work out how many litres of petrol you can buy for $85. . . . . . .

4 The equation of a straight line is $4x + 5y = 200$.

a Find the point where the line crosses the x-axis. . . . . . .

b Find the point where the line crosses the y-axis. . . . . . .

c Find the gradient of the line. . . . . . .

19 Interpreting and discussing results

19.1 Interpreting and drawing frequency diagrams

1 Sixty students were asked to solve a puzzle as quickly as possible. The time it took them, in seconds to the nearest second, was recorded. Here are the results.

| 20 | 44 | 34 | 50 | 33 | 41 | 38 | 43 | 53 | 35 | 47 | 40 | 27 | 49 | 24 |

| 35 | 39 | 21 | 38 | 36 | 23 | 32 | 30 | 40 | 35 | 25 | 32 | 47 | 33 | 48 |

| 45 | 30 | 41 | 33 | 49 | 37 | 54 | 47 | 34 | 45 | 36 | 56 | 35 | 58 | 40 |

| 20 | 51 | 31 | 26 | 39 | 30 | 41 | 35 | 54 | 37 | 46 | 22 | 42 | 31 | 29 |

a Draw a grouped frequency table for this data.
Decide on your own group intervals.
You do not need to use all the rows in the table.

> Find the quickest and slowest times first. This will help you decide on the group intervals.

Time to solve puzzle, t (seconds)	Tally	Frequency	Midpoint

b Draw a frequency polygon to show the data. Remember to include a title and to label the axes.

c Make one comment about what your polygon tells you about the time it took the students to complete the puzzle.

....

....

19.2 Interpreting and drawing line graphs

1 The table shows the exchange rate of US dollars ($) into UK pounds (£) on the same day each month over a six-month period.

Month	Jan	Feb	Mar	Apr	May	Jun
Value of $1	£0.70	£0.74	£0.69	£0.67	£0.70	£0.77

a Draw a line graph to show this data.

> Start the vertical axis at £0.60 and use a scale of 10 small squares = £0.10.

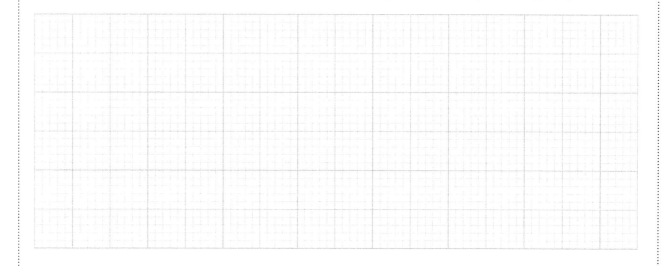

b Between which months was:

i the biggest increase in value? ....

ii the biggest decrease in value? ....

c Brad changed $1200 into pounds in February. How many pounds (£) did he get?

....

d Lisa changed £1400 into dollars in May. How many dollars ($) did she get?

....

e During which months was it best to change:

    i   dollars into pounds? Explain your answer.

        ....

        ....

    ii pounds into dollars? Explain your answer.

        ....

        ....

19.3 Interpreting and drawing scatter graphs

1 The scatter graph shows the algebra and geometry test results of 10 students. Both tests were marked out of 20.

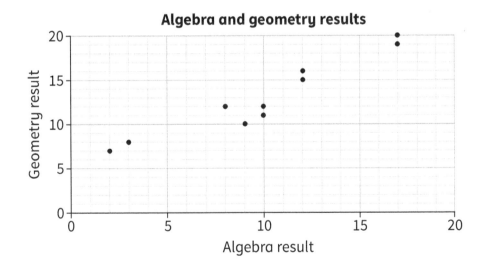

Algebra and geometry results

a Work out the mean algebra score.

....

b Work out the mean geometry score.

....

c Plot the mean point on the scatter graph with an X.

A line of best fit on a scatter graph is a straight line that passes through the mean point.

It also goes roughly through the middle of all the other points.

For example, for this data (X is the mean) the line of best fit could look like this:

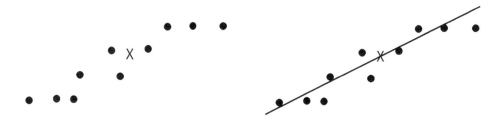

(d) On the graph on page 139, draw a line of best fit. Use your line of best fit to estimate:

i   the geometry score of a student who scored 6 in algebra.

    ....

ii   the algebra score of a student who scored 14 in geometry.

    ....

19.4 Interpreting and drawing stem-and-leaf diagrams

1 Oditi compares the heights of the students in classes 9T and 9R. She draws this back-to-back stem-and-leaf diagram to show her results.

Oditi also calculates the mean, median, mode and range for each class. Unfortunately Oditi has spilt tea on her work!

Heights of class 9T   Heights of class 9R

```
7  7  6  6  5  3  3  2  1  1  [stain] | 13 | 5  5  6  7  8  9
            9  7  6  5  4  1  0  0 | 14 | 0  1  1  2  4  5  [stain]  9  9  9
                        7  [stain]  2  2 | 15 | 0  0  1  7  8  [stain]
                  3  3  2  1  0  0 | 16 | 0  1
```

Key: 13|5 means 135 cm

	Range (cm)	Median height (cm)	Modal height (cm)	Mean height (cm)
Class 9T	33	[stain]	152	[stain]
Class 9R	30	145	[stain]	147

a Work out the numbers under the tea stains.

....

....

....

....

....

....

....

b Compare and comment on the heights of the students in classes 9T and 9R.

....

....

....

....

19.5 Comparing distributions and drawing conclusions

1 The pie charts show the ages of patients at two different dental surgeries.

Los Narejos dental surgery   **Los Arcos dental surgery**

Age (years)
- 0–20
- 21–40
- 41–60
- Over 60

a) Which surgery has:

i the greatest proportion of patients aged over 60?

....

ii the smallest proportion of patients aged 20 and under?

....

Los Narejos surgery has 1800 patients. Los Arcos surgery has 2880 patients.

b) Which surgery has:

i the greatest number of patients aged over 60?

....

ii the smallest number of patients aged 20 and under?

....

c) Explain why your answers to parts a) and b) are not the same.

....

Mixed questions

1 The line graph shows the wheat prices in the USA on the same day each month over one year. The prices are given in cents per bushel (c/bu).

> A bushel is a measurement used in the USA. 1 tonne ≈ 36.7 bushels.

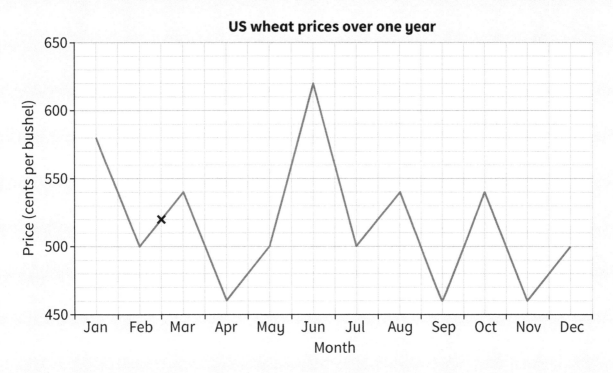

US wheat prices over one year

(a) Complete the table showing the monthly wheat prices.

Month	Jan	Feb	Mar	Apr	May	Jun	Jul	Aug	Sep	Oct	Nov	Dec
Wheat price (c/bu)	580											

(b) To get a more accurate idea of the trend in the prices you can use a moving average.

Follow and complete these steps to find the moving averages over 4 months.

Step 1: Find the average price for January, February, March and April:
(580 + 500 + 540 + 460) ÷ 4 = 520.

Step 2: Plot this point on the graph half way between February and March (shown by an X).

Step 3: Find the average price for February, March, April and May:
(500 + 540 + 460 + 500) ÷ 4 = ...

Step 4: Plot this point on the graph half way between March and April.

Step 5: Complete this table to work out all nine moving averages. Plot them all on the graph.

Moving average four months	Jan Feb Mar Apr	Feb Mar Apr May	Mar Apr May Jun		
Average price (c/bu)	520				
Plot between	Feb & Mar	Mar & Apr	Apr & May		

Moving average four months				
Average price (c/bu)				
Plot between				

c Join the moving averages on your graph with straight lines. What does the moving averages line graph tell you about the overall trend in wheat prices?

....

....